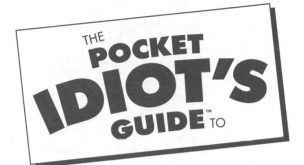

THE POCKET IDIOT'S GUIDE TO

Potty Training Problems

*by Alison D. Schonwald, M.D., FAAP
and George G. Sheldon*

D0111333

ALPHA

A member of Penguin Group (USA) Inc.

ALPHA BOOKS

Published by the Penguin Group

Penguin Group (USA) Inc., 375 Hudson Street, New York, New York 10014, U.S.A.

Penguin Group (Canada), 10 Alcorn Avenue, Toronto, Ontario, Canada M4V 3B2 (a division of Pearson Penguin Canada Inc.)

Penguin Books Ltd, 80 Strand, London WC2R 0RL, England

Penguin Ireland, 25 St Stephen's Green, Dublin 2, Ireland (a division of Penguin Books Ltd)

Penguin Group (Australia), 250 Camberwell Road, Camberwell, Victoria 3124, Australia (a division of Pearson Australia Group Pty Ltd)

Penguin Books India Pvt Ltd, 11 Community Centre, Panchsheel Park, New Delhi— 110 017, India

Penguin Group (NZ), cnr Airborne and Rosedale Roads, Albany, Auckland 1310, New Zealand (a division of Pearson New Zealand Ltd)

Penguin Books (South Africa) (Pty) Ltd, 24 Sturdee Avenue, Rosebank, Johannesburg 2196, South Africa

Penguin Books Ltd, Registered Offices: 80 Strand, London WC2R 0RL, England

International Standard Book Number: 1-59257-517-X
Library of Congress Catalog Card Number: 2005938290

08 07 06   8 7 6 5 4 3 2

Interpretation of the printing code: The rightmost number of the first series of numbers is the year of the book's printing; the rightmost number of the second series of numbers is the number of the book's printing. For example, a printing code of 06-1 shows that the first printing occurred in 2006.

Printed in the United States of America

Note: This publication contains the opinions and ideas of its authors. It is intended to provide helpful and informative material on the subject matter covered. It is sold with the understanding that the authors and publisher are not engaged in rendering professional services in the book. If the reader requires personal assistance or advice, a competent professional should be consulted.

The authors and publisher specifically disclaim any responsibility for any liability, loss, or risk, personal or otherwise, which is incurred as a consequence, directly or indirectly, of the use and application of any of the contents of this book.

Most Alpha books are available at special quantity discounts for bulk purchases for sales promotions, premiums, fund-raising, or educational use. Special books, or book excerpts, can also be created to fit specific needs.

For details, write: Special Markets, Alpha Books, 375 Hudson Street, New York, NY 10014.

Contents

Introduction

Have you started potty training your child, but it isn't going too well? Do your neighbors and relatives tell stories of training their kids in a day, but your kid has been sitting on the potty for months without producing a thing? Or maybe your child has used the toilet a few times, but now folds his arms and refuses to enter the bathroom no matter how much you beg. If so, don't worry! This book is for you.

No matter what the issue with your reluctant potty user, you'll become an expert at training your child. This book is stuffed full of ideas, insight, tips, and techniques you can use to turn your child into a potty-using pro.

Potty training can be intimidating, for you and for your child. You probably never imagined you'd seek help for this normal developmental step, and are probably not thrilled to be thinking about poop and pee all the time, let alone cleaning it up.

This book helps set things straight, and tells you what to do, and not to do, to help your child through the process. We've eliminated the big medical terms, and instead offer you practical advice in easy-to-understand, practical terms. Though it's hard to believe right now, pretty soon you'll learn how to excite your child about this new skill: using the potty.

Extras

In addition to the main text, this book includes three kinds of sidebars, each with a distinctive visual cue:

Potty Do's

These tips will give you fresh ideas or special information to help you train your reluctant child.

Potty Don'ts

These are warnings and cautions, to help you understand what not to do while potty training.

Training Trivia

These are additional bits of information, things you probably don't know, but they're added to give you more details about potty training.

Acknowledgments

For Seth, my husband and best friend, and with thanks to Leonard Rappaport and my colleagues in the Developmental Medicine Center at Children's Hospital, Boston.

Both authors would like to thank their literary agent, Robert G. Diforio of the D4EO Literary Agency, for his patience and repeated efforts in arranging this project for us.

Trademarks

Why Is My Child So Reluctant?

In This Chapter

- Are you and your child ready?
- Understanding your child's reluctance
- Problems that might be preventing your success
- Recognizing constipation and urinary issues

It's time for that toddler of yours to reach one of life's milestones: potty training. Many of his friends and cousins are well on their way, but your child seems hesitant, dragging his feet, or perhaps he downright refuses. When you bring up the topic or try to escort him to the bathroom to sit on the toilet, he balks, says he's too busy, or runs in the opposite direction. If you persist … a temper tantrum erupts.

While you've heard that you shouldn't push it, it's really hard not to. You try to let him take his time, but how much time will he take? You feel you need to be doing something to get the potty training program underway. But what? This chapter will help you identify potty training obstacles and understand why your child might be so reluctant.

Potty Patience

There have been some signs of interest. Your child may have watched a sibling using the potty, and imitates that child in every other way. Maybe the child has even tried to use the toilet once or twice. You think your normally curious little one should be ready. Why not? Your child seems advanced in other areas, maybe speaking better than peers, taking every toy apart and putting it back together, remembering things that even you can't. But the moment you say "potty," your little one screams and runs away, determined not to use anything other than familiar diapers.

Maybe your child is ready … or maybe not.

To make matters worse, you feel pressure to get your child potty trained. Whether from your mother-in-law or neighbors (the perfect parents with the perfect children), the pressure is turning to stress. With preschool a few months in the future and the requirement that children must be potty trained, you're concerned and maybe a touch panicked. Don't worry. In these pages are the advice and guidance you will need to move your little one from diapers to underwear.

Take a deep breath and relax. First things first: it's important to realize that learning to use the toilet may not be an instant, overnight, or one-day process. Indeed, it takes at least a few weeks for most toddlers and several months for others to become competent staying clean and dry and using the toilet.

And for some toddlers, it takes weeks just to warm up to the idea of trying. Other than time, it will take lots of patience, and if you picked up this book, likely some new strategies on your part. There will be accidents, messes, and times when you doubt that your child will ever be potty trained. You'll fear that your child will indeed be packing diapers when he goes off to college.

Did you catch that part about potty training taking a lot of patience? You will soon think this is the biggest understatement you ever read. You may feel frustrated, annoyed, embarrassed, and even angry at times. But then a breakthrough moment will occur when your child marches into the bathroom and performs on the toilet. Then a few days will slip by with no successes or interest at all. One day it will be over, your child will use the toilet with proficiency, and you'll forget all the irritations along the way.

But for now, your child is reluctant to begin (or continue) with potty training. Why? There are many reasons—sometimes obvious, sometimes not.

Is Your Child Too Young?

Many toddlers between the ages of 18 and 22 months begin to show interest in toileting. Some may even have a few successes on the toilet. You'll get excited, believing that your child is precocious and that toilet training will be a breeze. You even do a little bragging to family members and friends.

Then as fast as the process got underway, your child loses interest. It was too much work. Your young toddler simply has other activities that hold his interest and satisfy his curiosity far more than using the toilet. For now, it takes too much work and concentration.

His body, mind, and emotions may not be ready for the challenge. Perhaps he's focusing his energy on other new skills. His language is improving, his running is better coordinated, and he's doing many things on his own. He may have explored the idea of toilet training, but it was really just a false start. While he isn't ready, he's interested.

Don't start your child too soon. You do best by your toddler if you follow his lead, support his level of interest in potty training, and wait until his second birthday and then begin to look for signs of readiness. If you push it now, your child might become more reluctant when he could actually be learning to use the toilet regularly. Most toddlers under two years old have other things on their minds than officially learning to use the toilet.

Toddler Independence

Why did Mother Nature do this to parents? Just when the terrible twos take hold, when toddlers go out of their way to assert their independence, they also must learn to use the toilet. They're affirming their autonomy by proving they have a mind of their own. If you say "yes," they say "no."

If you say, "Do you want to go to the potty?" the response may be a resounding, "NO!" Most self-respecting toddlers who are out to establish their sovereignty from you will say "no" to your ideas about using the toilet, especially if you're making unrealistic demands.

That's why it's your job to work around this natural tendency to be oppositional. Instead of asking for your child's preference and giving your child an easy chance to refuse, you might choose to say, "It's time to sit on the potty," or "It's time to practice." Compliance just because mom and dad said so isn't part of the toddler modus operandi.

The Story of Nicky No: Nicky was a sweet one-year-old who became an entirely new child upon turning two. The agreeable infant who smiled at every turn before his second birthday became a screaming speed-demon with a mind of his own. Angelic cooing was replaced with phrases like "It's mine!" and "Not you!" at every opportunity. Nicky's mother knew that if she suggested he use the potty, Nicky would answer with his familiar refusal. Waiting for him to show interest in the toilet, Nicky's mother tried to stop saying no herself, whenever she could. She finally bought a potty chair, and stopped herself from asking Nicky if he wanted to use it. On his own, Nicky started sitting on the little chair. His mother showed her approval with big smiles and happy winks, but never gave Nicky No the chance to use his favorite words.

Difficult Temperament

Some children are reluctant to train just because of their personal styles. They tend to respond to life's challenges with less ease than more mellow kids might. Medical studies that compare groups of children who had trouble training with others who trained easily show a difference in temperament.

Difficult toilet trainers are more likely to be "less adaptable," meaning that when they're in new places and with new people, they have more trouble adjusting. They may not like changes in routine, and aren't likely to rush into new or dangerous situations.

As a group, reluctant trainers are more negative. They tend to do more crying and whining than easily trained children. This does not mean they're unhappy! Negative children aren't necessarily sad—they may just see the glass as half empty, or they may be the serious and thoughtful types.

The difficult child—the one described as a difficult trainer—tends to be less persistent and becomes frustrated. They give up more easily when things don't go well. They're more likely to withdraw from a new situation rather than readily accept it. They're often hesitant and resistant, and think very carefully before they act.

Your child may not be a difficult child in general. In fact, most children who struggle to train aren't really "difficult children." They're no more intense, disruptive, naughty, mean, or hurtful than anyone else their age. Their cautious approach and preference for routine may make them safer and more predictable than children who are more laid back.

Unfortunately, when faced with the challenge to start using the toilet, their difficult temperamental traits may kick in, making it harder to approach and stick with this new expectation.

Other Obstacles

While trying to achieve your goal—potty training that reluctant child of yours—you might find there are other problems that are preventing your success. They vary from child to child. For example, your child might be …

- resistant to change.
- afraid of the toilet.
- anxious about a new sibling.
- dependent on Pull-Ups.
- held back by cumbersome clothing.
- busy playing.
- affected by busy parents.

Resisting Change

Some kids resist the toilet because they never had to do it before. This may be the child who wants the same breakfast every day, won't eat anything green, and wants only mommy to put her to bed. Sameness can be reassuring to kids. It helps them know that their world is safe and predictable.

The ideas of not having the diaper, making bowel movements in the bathroom, not getting changed through the day, and so on, may just be completely unappealing. This is downright frightening compared to what they already know. Their resistance might just be a natural defense.

Fear of the Toilet

While many toddlers are highly interested and curious about the toilet, many fear that when pee and poop go down the toilet, they might, too. It's scary when something disappears, and the child has no idea where it goes. Toddlers live in the here and now—what is in front of them is what is real. They can't see under the bed or in the closet, and fear the monsters that may be there. So too, that unknown place where items go when flushed may bring magical fears and make kids anxious. Their perception is skewed.

You might need to kneel down next to the toilet, surround your child with your arms, and reassure her that you aren't going to allow her to be flushed away. You can tell her that all of the poops and pees will be together and safe, and she will stay here and be safe.

Potty Do's

Allow your child to flush for you and other members of the family. As gross as it sounds, most toddlers like to see the pee and poop go down the toilet and by doing so they overcome their fears that they might be flushed away, too, and they become more accustomed to the mysterious disappearance.

New Sibling

If there is a new sibling in the house, everything gets turned upside down. With the arrival of a sibling, potty training often takes a back seat. Other issues—like just managing life with the competition a new baby brings—must take precedence.

The sibling's arrival can cause regression or delays in potty training, and in other developmental skills as well. If parents push it, resistance from the toddler can escalate.

Think about it. Let's say your husband announces that his best friend from high school is moving in with the two of you. You'd be a little annoyed, maybe jealous, and fearful. He would disrupt your routines, add a new element to household decisions, and take away your husband's attention. You may be happy to have him around sometimes, but other times he would be a real nuisance! If you'd just learned to use a complicated computer program, your attention and organization when using this new skill might regress as you adjust to the idea of this new person in your home.

Although siblings are accepted practice and hosting a fraternity in your home isn't, most first-born children feel similarly regarding the intrusion of a baby sister or brother. Any new skill, particularly learning to use the toilet, might fall by the wayside until parents' words and actions reassure the child that he's still loved and an important member of the family.

The newly trained child will most likely experience a setback until life as the dethroned older brother or sister settles in. It usually takes three weeks to three months to adjust to life with the new baby. That's when it's your cue to begin training anew.

Dependence on Pull-Ups

Many parents move their children into disposable training pants (known as Pull-Ups), mistakenly believing that this alone will inspire the child to use the toilet. It just doesn't work this way. Disposable or cotton training pants are only a temporary fix that can sometimes lead to a dependency on the training pants rather than a tool to use on the road to successes on the toilet. Many of the disposable training pants do their job too well.

Because of these pants, children often don't learn the difference between clean and dirty, and wet and dry. A toddler needs the opportunity to learn these differences. They learn this when wearing lightweight cotton underwear with a training pant or rubber pant over their panties. Doing so gives children the opportunity to feel the sensation of having pee and poop in the pants ... typically an unpleasant feeling.

When they realize what's happening with their body, then they're more able to control their bowels and bladder. (There will be much more about when to use Pull-Ups in Chapter 5.)

Cumbersome Clothing

If your child wears overalls or pants with a zipper, belt, and snap, using the toilet might just be too much trouble. Your child might be resistant just because of his or her clothing. Eliminate the hassle by putting your son in sweat pants and your daughter in a dress. You will learn more about this in Chapter 5.

Busy Playing

It might be perfectly obvious that your child needs to use the toilet but does not want to stop playing. Play is an important part of any busy toddler's day. See Chapter 5 for tips and ideas on how to handle interrupting playtime to get your toddler to sit on the toilet.

Busy Parents

Most parents today are on the go (you probably are, too). Many work outside the home, all work inside the home, and their children are involved in a variety of activities—music, gymnastics, sports, and playgroups. With older siblings heading off to soccer, scouts, and piano lessons, the younger ones may be easier to handle in diapers than underwear. You might be just too busy to give potty training the attention it needs. This could be a troublesome issue that is making your child more reluctant.

A new baby might be on the way, or there may be travel, family weddings, or an extended house-guest. Any of these events could delay teaching your toddler to use the toilet. Will life ever settle down enough to provide a calm, relaxed few weeks to get the process underway? Possibly, if there's a snowstorm and you're house-bound for weeks. This likely won't be the case, so you're going to have to work toilet-teaching into your rigorous schedule or give up something to make time for it.

This busy lifestyle makes it tough. Sometimes, it's easier maintain the status quo. It isn't that you don't want to get the child on the road to toilet training, it's just that you don't have the time or energy to get it started.

While busyness is a reason to hold off on the challenges of teaching your child to use the toilet, it's not an excuse. At some point, you'll need to grasp hold of the toilet training reins and get it underway.

Maybe It's Something Else

There are several other reasons why your child might seem reluctant and fails to train as easily as you were expecting. For example, you need to rule out constipation and urinary tract infections:

- **Constipation.** Your child could be constipated. After all, if it hurts to go, your child won't want to go. Who can blame the kid? Until the constipation is treated, you're unlikely to make much progress. Your child might be constipated if poops are hard, huge, or they hurt. (For more information about constipation, see Chapter 8.)

- **Urinary tract infections.** Urinary tract infections are more common in girls. Uncontrollable urine can be one symptom, and pain when peeing can be another. All children with pee accidents beyond the age of expected training should have a simple urine test at the doctor's office.

For all late trainers, it's worth mentioning your concern to your child's doctor, who can make sure that no medical problems are causing the delay.

> **Training Trivia**
>
> A urinary tract infection (UTI) is a bacterial infection in the child's urine, causing the bladder to spasm and squeeze out urine without warning. Other signs of a UTI are strong or foul-smelling urine, burning when peeing, and peeing that's more frequent than usual. Oral antibiotics are usually effective treatment.

The Least You Need to Know

- Follow your toddler's lead by supporting his level of interest in potty training, and wait until his second birthday to look for signs of readiness.

- Children can become reluctant to potty train because of their need for independence or simply as an expression of their temperament.

- There can be numerous unintentional obstacles that make your toddler reluctant to potty train.

- A child reluctant to potty train could have medical problems like constipation or a urinary tract infection.

Chapter 2

What Am I Doing Wrong?

In This Chapter

- When training doesn't fit into your lifestyle
- What words to use and how to use them
- How to change your child's refusal without him knowing it

Your child just won't toilet train. While you naturally will be looking at your child as the problem, maybe at least part of the focus should be on you. Sooner or later, you're likely to wonder what *you* might be doing wrong. So in this chapter, we'll explore the possibility of the solution to potty training your reluctant child resting with you.

Busy, Busy, Busy

Parents today are busy. Many work outside their home and, of course, all work inside their home caring for their children and keeping up with household tasks.

It seems, too, that children today are more scheduled than ever before, going to preschool and various other activities. How do parents even begin to find the time, energy, and concentration to teach their child to use the toilet?

Somehow, you need to find the focus in your daily activities. While you don't have to give up your life to start and follow through with potty training, you do need to include it in your lifestyle.

Slowing Your Life Down

Take a deep breath, relax, and realize you can do it. Consider making some changes to your daily schedule, for example:

- **Enlist the help of other family members or friends.** If you're going to establish a potty sit-down time before bed, then Dad may need to take over the bedtime routine for the other kids.

- **Make mealtimes easier with simple recipes.** If you need to be in the bathroom to reassure your child, then you can't be preparing a fancy meal at the same time. Frozen dinners can sometimes be delicious!

- **Reduce the number of errands you need to run during the day.** You need to be near the bathroom your child is comfortable using, so long afternoons running errands just won't work. You'll need to get as much done as you can while the kids are at playgroups or after they're asleep.

- **Let go of other daytime tasks for the next few months.** Explain to your friends that entertaining, talking on the phone, and watching TV will have to be on the back burner for a while.

Why? Because you want to introduce and support your child's toilet training in a regular but relaxed manner.

Your goal is to have her using the toilet several times throughout the day. However, if you're rushed or distracted, this new activity will feel more stressful, and for your reluctant child, you want to avoid any stress associated with toileting.

 Potty Do's

Make the adjustments to your schedule as necessary. Remember, this will be temporary, and not a permanent change.

Potty training must now become part of the daily schedule. From your own announcements of "I have to use the potty" to the practice time of your toddler sitting on the potty chair, all this now needs to be moved to the top of your priority list.

Working It into the Daily Routine

Toddlers (as well as older children) rely on their schedules and regular routines. One big reason children are reluctant to learn to use the potty is that it has not been part of their regular schedule. Potty has never before been a part of getting up in the morning, going down for a nap, getting out the door, taking a bath, or going to bed. Here's an opportunity for change, but one that you will have to instill.

Start with routine events in your child's day such as getting in the bathtub and getting out the door to go somewhere. For example, tell your child that from now on, "We're going to sit on the toilet before getting in the bathtub."

Potty Do's

Start with one time, such as after dinner. Have your child sit every day at that time. Read books, sing songs, make it fun. Every few days or each week, add another sit-down time.

You want to make the potty a safe and fun place to be. If you still sense resistance on your child's part, explain that this is just practice sitting, no poop or pee has to come out yet.

To work a practice sit-down time into the daily routine, toilet times have to fit naturally into your day. Here are some times that might work:

- After breakfast
- Before leaving in the morning

- After a nap
- After lunch
- Before getting into the car
- While mom makes dinner
- After dinner
- Before a bath
- After a bath
- During nighttime wash-up

Sitting times after meals can be really successful. They take into account the child's natural reflex to poop about a half hour after a meal.

Sit-down times that take place before leaving the house can take advantage of using siblings as role models. Point out to the toilet-training child that everyone is using the bathroom before getting into the car, so it's clearly not a punishment but rather a normal part of life.

Potty Do's

Keep in mind that in the beginning, performance isn't important, only working the process into your daily routine.

Potty Books and Videos

For most children, reading and watching videos are part of their regular activities. To normalize the process of learning to use the toilet, purchase books and DVDs that focus on potty training. By doing so, your child becomes more familiar with potty training. Without any interruption in your daily pattern, toileting is introduced and re inforced. If you read to your child before bed every night, be sure to include a toileting book. If your children watch videos while you make dinner, put in a fun toilet training one. You can borrow the books and DVDs from your local library.

Although books and DVDs alone won't inspire the child to use the toilet, it's helpful to incorporate them into the actual toilet training process. If your child has a favorite book, read it each time he sits on the toilet. You may even keep it there as an incentive to be in the bathroom.

Books and DVDs are astonishing adjuncts to the discussions you have with your toddler about toileting. Your child will become informed from your reading the book and by watching the DVDs. She finds out that she's not the only one who needs to learn to use the toilet, but that all children who have reached her age learn this, too.

Children's books about toileting are found in every bookstore, or are easily borrowed from the library. There are storybooks about children who learn to use the toilet. There are books that explain just what's happening with the body with waste and elimination. Some books include animals and their pooping, and some books have video options.

Potty Do's

Place potty training books in a basket near the toilet. You can read one to your child as he attempts to use the toilet, or watch the video as he prepares for his toilet use.

Everyone Does It

You need to change the toilet training dynamic, if it has reached explosive proportions for the particularly reluctant child and understandably flustered parent.

Rather than toilet training being something that "mommy wants me to do," the child learns that these are things everybody does. Your goal is for the child to get trained, but once the emotions flare, your child's resistance may be more about disagreeing with you than about refusing to use the toilet. When they learn other kids use the bathroom, their perspective may change.

As your child watches other children or characters undergo the same learning process, it will assist your toddler in understanding the whole toilet process. These tools can assist you with reinforcing the new ideas you have discussed, without the battles that may tend to start.

Reluctant Parent

Some parents don't know where to begin—
especially if it's a first child. They fear the messes,
apprehension, and bother. Some are truly disgusted
by the mess, and then feel guilty since it's from
their own child. They fear they'll do it wrong,
scarring the child for life. They don't want to deal
with the frustrations on their part or on the part
of their child. Also, parents are given mixed messages. Should they be pushing the child to train,
or letting the child indicate when she's ready?

Often, it seems that it's just easier to use a disposable diaper, change the child, and be done with it.
For the short term, that is fine. But in each child's
own way and time he needs to learn to use the
toilet. Parents need to expect it of their child and
make it a priority for the child who is ready to
learn.

Parent's Influence, Child's Control

Most children train between two and three years of
age. Their bodies, minds, emotions, and even their
social awareness have developed to the point where
they're perfectly able to learn to use the toilet.

Some learn between 3 and 3½ years of age. If the
parents wait much longer than that to start the
training task, the child may learn to live his life
in diapers or disposable training pants. She can
become well accustomed to them. The habit of

peeing and pooping in diapers might be long established, and then hard to break.

Parents want to do all they can to prevent this from occurring. Teaching a child over age 3½ to use the toilet is far more difficult than teaching a child between age 2 and 3.

Potty Don'ts

Even if you're dreading the stress of toilet training your child, try not to wait until 3½ to start training. At that point, the child has gotten used to wearing Pull-Ups and it might be harder to transition.

Parents use a variety of strategies to get toilet training started. The method usually reflects the parents' goals and style, and not necessarily the child's:

- Some parents take all diapers or disposable training pants away and deal with accidents until the child is willing to use the toilet. Children who are already stressed may be overwhelmed by such a severe intervention.

- Some parents allow the child to decide daily if he wants to wear underwear or training pants. For a child who does best with routine and structure, this can be disastrous!

- Some parents put the issue totally in the child's court, allowing the child to be completely in charge of the matter, knowing confidently that in the child's own way and time he'll learn. This may work for the self-directed and organized child, but usually needs some toileting successes to work.

All three approaches are typical of reluctant parents who are hoping that the child's agenda will match their own timetable. They assume that the child will train either because there is no option for diapers, or because the child is somehow internally motivated to train at his own pace.

What's missing in these methods, for many children, is the help they need from their parents in developing potty training skills and confidence. Some kids can train any way you try, but reluctant ones have declared that toilet training won't be so easy.

Don't Talk Too Much

Parents often try to convince their children to train. Here are some common attempts:

- "Don't you hate those dirty smelly diapers?"
- "Do you want to be more grown up?"
- "Don't you want to be like your big brother/sister?"
- "I'll give you a treat if you poop in the toilet!"

The reluctant child often answers back in a negative manner, leading to a lengthy discussion and negotiation. The conversation may go like this …

Parent: "Taylor, do you have to go? Why don't you make in the toilet?"

Taylor: "No, want to go here."

Parent: "But the toilet is where grown-ups go."

Taylor: "Me little."

Parent: "You won't go to preschool if you're wearing a diaper."

Taylor: "Why?"

Parent: "That's the rule."

Taylor: "Why?"

Parent: "The teacher made it."

Taylor: "Why?"

Parent: "Well, you'll make mommy so happy if you poop in the toilet. I'll give you a treat if you do!"

Taylor: "NOOOOOOOOOO!!!!!!!!!!!!!!!"

This discussion is too long! This is a toddler! It's hard, since you want to reason with your children and teach them how to make good decisions. You swore you wouldn't be like your parents, and when asked "why?" answer with, "because I said so."

One problem with too much conversation is that you're reinforcing your child's failure to use the toilet with too much attention. Attention itself can make the child want to continue refusing, because often the parental time and energy can be the reward.

The child can get you running in circles and your brain spinning to make a convincing argument. Take a step back and realize that the reluctant child's resistance isn't based on lack of believing in the need to train. A formal debate won't change your child's attitude about training and then get your child where he needs to be. Rather, recognize what the actual obstacles for that child are; refer to Chapter 1 if you need reminding.

A Battle You Won't Win

Rational thinking is how adults make decisions—young children are far less complex in their thought processes. Lengthy conversations about potty training will actually make things worse.

The child is already reluctant, because of innate temperament, lack of developmental skills, too many other changes going on, or lack of interest, to name a few. Extended discussion will just add to the pressure and make training even harder to do.

The goal is to use neutral comments that encourage without pressuring the child. Here are some examples:

Uses Pressure	Uses Encouragement
You have to go, you've done it before.	I know you can go, you've done it before.
Why can't you do it again?	I know you can do it again.
Everyone else is trained.	You can learn this when you're ready.

There is a limit to the encouragement you give. Signs that even your most supportive attempts are felt as stressful to your child can be hard to read. If your child sometimes makes an effort to do the toileting task, then keep moving in the training direction. However, if you see tears, tantrums, or terror with even the most gentle prodding, then think about backing off. See the end of Chapter 6 if you're thinking about this.

Keep an Upbeat Attitude

In your effort to encourage, it helps to talk about the successes in front of the child. Remind him that "we always use the bathroom before getting into the car" and don't forget to congratulate him when he does so.

Don't discuss the setbacks or problems the same way. If concerns must be discussed, use e-mail or only speak of problems on the phone when the child is asleep or out of earshot. Remember how smart your child is; if she senses that the grown-ups are stressed or discouraged about her toileting, she will feel it, too, and may shy away from the challenge. Everyone needs to keep an upbeat and positive attitude.

Consistency Counts

Your child's day might take her to a number of different locations. She may start in your home, go to morning preschool or daycare, spend a few afternoons each week at the grandparents' home, and the rest back with you. Your child might be hesitant to use the toilet because Dad's approach to potty training is different from Mom's. And then Grandma's method is different from the childcare provider's. And so on, and so on ….

The result is simple: your child gets easily mixed up, confused, and frustrated. Am I supposed to practice sitting or do they expect me to pee? Do I go to the bathroom alone or with someone? Do I wipe myself or can I get some help? You can imagine preferring to avoid the task altogether rather than attempting to figure out all of these answers.

Potty training can, by itself, be frustrating and all these different approaches add to it. What's a parent to do?

Consider where the child is throughout the day, and all of the adults and settings involved for the potty training child. You will need to communicate with one another about how training takes place at each location.

The discussion should include the successes that support the child on the road to potty training. For example:

- If the child does best with a footstool for support, then there should be a footstool at each location.
- If there is a book that Mom and Dad always read when the child sits on the toilet, then Grandma and the childcare provider might read it as well.
- If the rule is a sit-down time before getting into the car, then that rule should be enforced at each different location.

Although all the adults need to do their best to be on the same potty training page, it's impossible to be exactly the same as one another. Take heart—you're not doomed, and neither is the child. Children are capable of learning that at Grandma's house we use the toilet one way, at childcare another, and at home it's a little different. The whole process might take a bit longer, but in time the child will learn the procedures and approaches with each person and in each environment if consistency can't be assured.

But some key strategies should certainly be consistent. There can be no negativity or unrealistic expectations from any adults involved.

Potty Don'ts

All the involved adults need to know and be made aware that punishments, reprimands, and scolding aren't part of potty training.

When Your Child Flatly Refuses

Remember to avoid extensive negotiations with a refuser and that you can't convince him with reason and debate. You'll surprise your child by agreeing, in the most natural and calm manner you can manage. Here are a couple of examples:

- When a child refuses to sit on the toilet during a scheduled time, you can answer with, "Okay. Then no sticker tonight."
- A child who won't wipe when that was the job of the week can be handled with, "Okay. You're not ready to wipe tonight. Maybe you'll be ready tomorrow."

When your child flatly refuses to use the potty, think of this as an opportunity to find a common ground.

No! You Can't Make Me!

Some children will really protest. A nod of the head or failure to try may turn into a loud shout, like, "No! You can't make me!"

The child is telling you she needs to have some control over this situation, so it's important to give that child some control. When kids have control, they're less resistant.

What control can you give her? Start by allowing the hesitant child to make a decision whenever you can. For example, if sitting can take place before or after bath time, let the child choose which one. He can decide which book to read during the sit-down time, or she can choose which bathroom in the house to use.

Here are some choices you may give your child so he feels more in control of the sit-down experience:

- With underwear/Pull-Ups or naked?
- Toilet seat cover up or down?
- Which book? (give specific choices, so "none" isn't an option)
- Which song? (again, specific choices)
- Sit for 4 minutes or 5 minutes?
- Which sticker to earn for sitting?

 Training Trivia

Children tend to be most relaxed after a bath. For the anxious child, toileting after bath time can be a good choice.

Accentuate the Positive

In all cases, notice that accentuating the positive is effective. Think of your own workplace. A financial reward motivates us to work harder, while the threat of a salary cut just makes us worried, angry, and resentful. Every toileting comment can be rephrased from bad to good, from a failure to a success. Just getting into the bathroom is a step toward training that can be praised.

Eliminate the Negative

Eliminating the negative will help your child in toilet training and in meeting all of life's challenges. The goal is to feel successful and confident, so that we can face harder goals rather than run the other way. Toileting is an area with particular risk for too much negativity. It's hard not to yell and show your frustration with the child, but do your best to hide it.

Some parents strike their child, or at least are tempted to do so, in the escalations around toileting that commonly occur. If you're feeling this angry, take a break. Put yourself in time-out to cool off, and rethink your approach and how it's working. Also, see Chapter 10 for more thoughts about eliminating the negative.

The Least You Need to Know

- Toilet training has to be a relaxed process where the parents influence, but cannot control, the outcome.

- Helping your child train requires few words, but lots of encouragement and positive reinforcement.

- Behavior changes are easier to make when we work for rewards rather than try to avoid punishment.

3

Inspiring the Reluctant Child

As you plan the potty training of your reluctant child, one of your best first steps is to find ways to inspire your son or daughter. Getting them interested in the idea of using the potty is often the key to getting toddlers to use the toilet.

In this chapter, you will learn some simple and easy ways to inspire your child. Using these techniques can make the potty training chore easier on you and your child.

Making the Bathroom Appealing

In many homes, children inadvertently get the message that the bathroom is off limits. Parents don't mean for this to happen. After all, many households keep the bathroom door closed whether in use or not, so children may get the impression the bathroom is not a room for them to use.

When adults use the bathroom, they typically close the door to get some privacy and a little alone time. When you do this, your child may get the message that—other than for taking a bath—the bathroom isn't for them. Importantly, your child might have no idea what else happens in the bathroom other than taking a bath!

Most likely, you've changed your child's diapers on a changing table in their bedroom, so use of the toilet by you or others could seem as if it's a "for adults only" activity. If this is the impression your child is receiving, it's time to embrace an open door bathroom policy. Shed your modesty, at least in front of your child, and make the bathroom an everyday part of your household that your toddler accesses several times a day.

Now is a good time to get your child familiar and comfortable with the bathroom. Some things you can do to make sure your little one feels welcome in the bathroom include:

- Keep the bathroom door open and accessible unless you have household guests.

- Allow your child to wander in and out of the bathroom when you brush your teeth, take a bath, and use the toilet.

- Have your child assist you in restocking the bathroom with fresh towels and washcloths.

- Allow your child to help carry toilet paper rolls to the bathroom as needed.

- Make an extra effort to wash dirty hands in the bathroom—rather than the kitchen.

- Spend extra time in the bathroom brushing teeth or taking baths, and in time sitting on the toilet to practice toileting.

Just as your child has access to the kitchen, family room, and his bedroom, you want him to feel like the bathroom is one of his accessible rooms as well. Spending some extra time in the bathroom is a good way to get your child familiar and comfortable in the room.

This room is like no other. It has an exhaust fan, shiny (and often cold) floor, running water, a shower curtain, and a strange chair that flushes, that until now, your child may have been told not to touch.

To some children, it might seem strange, something to be avoided. You or your spouse may have even said, "Get out! I need some privacy." Even if you haven't said that, your child can tell if you feel that way.

Potty Do's _____

For the reluctant child, making the bathroom appealing may mean keeping a favorite toy there. If he can only play with his favorite train or her favorite markers on the bathroom floor, then he or she will learn to associate bathroom time with fun activities.

Cultivating Interest

Creating interest about toileting with your toddler is as easy as talking about it. Normalize it as part of what big people do in their everyday lives, like sleeping and eating.

Say things to your child like, "I'm going into the bathroom. I need to pee." Or, "Grandma is going into the bathroom. It's her turn to use the toilet." You tell your child when it's time to eat, when you're going to get a pair of socks, and when it's bedtime. Announcing toilet time will normalize using the toilet and make it less of an overwhelming and out-of-the-ordinary new task.

Don't make using the toilet an isolated experience. Show your child the bathrooms in both friends' and relatives' homes. Let your child realize that toilets are everywhere because everyone uses them everyday. Once kids are trained, they often are hesitant to go anywhere other than at home.

Introducing them just for fun, without expecting your child to use a foreign bathroom, will make using strange toilets less scary in the future.

Another effective way to explain the process is with animals. Explain about the places where animals pee and poop. Tell your child that when animals pee and poop, they just do it where they are: bears go in the woods, squirrels go in the park, and birds make poops when they're flying in the air! Little animals have tiny poops, elephants have giant ones. Make it a fun discussion—keep the tone matter of fact, reminding your child that it is normal to pee and poop. When considering all the places different animals go, remind your child that birds may go in the air but people use the toilet.

Shopping for Underpants

Plan a special shopping trip with your child. Allow your son or daughter to choose his or her underwear.

By involving your child in the underwear selection and buying process, you give the child control in the situation. Use this as a simple yet effective way to draw him into the major change of going from diapers to training pants to lightweight cotton underwear.

Picking the Potty

You can also engage your child's interest in potty training by letting her help choose a potty chair. There are many different styles and types available.

You'll do best by your child if you involve her in the potty chair shopping spree. If there is something your child does not like about the potty chair, there could be resistance to using it.

You need to purchase a potty chair or a child-sized potty seat that securely and correctly fits over the toilet seat. The stand-alone, toddler-sized potty chair with a bowl that can be emptied into the toilet is standard.

Imagine you're sitting on a giant-sized toilet, whose bowl is huge compared to your own bottom, with your legs dangling in the air, several feet off the ground. Would you feel relaxed enough to urinate or defecate? Or would you be holding on for dear life? With that in mind, here are some things to consider:

- The potty chair often makes sense, especially if you believe your child might be scared of or have trouble sitting on the adult-sized toilet.

- Make sure any child-sized seat designed to fit over the regular toilet seat is secure and does not wobble. The last thing you want is for the seat to shift around and make your child feel insecure or afraid that he or she will fall into the toilet.

- It may make the most sense to buy both—start your child potty training on the potty chair, and then move to the potty seat on the adult toilet.

- When your child starts to use the big toilet, dangling legs can add to the feeling of instability. A small footstool, stack of telephone books, or upside down garbage pail can be useful to increase your child's feeling of security.

You don't need to spend a fortune on a potty chair, but make sure that it's well built. Also, be certain the "pot" part (where the pee and poop end up) of the potty chair easily empties for quick cleaning and minimal spilling.

Potty chairs are available in many different styles. One is available that is described as funny and includes big eyes. Your child may think it's funny—or scary. Avoid any chair style that might cause stress to your child.

Training Trivia

Some children love arts and crafts. To make her toilet more appealing and special, your child can decorate her new potty by painting it as a special activity. Kids can decorate potties with favorite stickers, too.

Potty Seat Considerations

If your house has many bathrooms, you'll need to decide just how many potty chairs and seats to purchase. While you don't need to buy a potty chair for every bathroom in your home, you may need one for the upstairs and one for the downstairs bathrooms. Or you need one for the bathroom near the child's area during the day and another near the child's bedroom for use in the morning or before going to bed at night.

Most children that begin potty training start with a potty chair. If your child is older—closer to 3 years old or older—or has an older sibling, the child might prefer to use the "real" toilet first. In this case, a child-sized seat, which fits over the toilet, is most helpful.

Stability of the seat is always important when picking a potty seat. When shopping, find one that is sturdy and has minimal jiggle.

Potty Don'ts _____

Make certain that any child-sized seat designed to fit over the adult toilet seat does not feel like it's going to collapse or give way under the weight of the child.

The child-sized seat should also be free from any parts that may pinch your child. Make sure there are no sharp edges. Carefully check the fit of the seat. If you have a padded seat on your toilet, the child-sized seat may not fit as securely. Your job is to do all you can to make sure your child feels secure while sitting on the potty seat.

Potty Portability

You may need to buy a portable potty or adapter to take on the road. Many stores have toilet seat adapters that fold up. You can slip it into your diaper bag. These portable potty seats are a wonderful option when using public rest rooms where sanitation is sometimes iffy. However, as terrific as they sound, some children will refuse to sit on these unfamiliar portable potty seats. Toddlers like familiar objects, activities, and people. If this is the case with your child, you might need to haul along their own potty chair.

If you have a van, it's easy for the child to just sit on his potty and go when the car is parked. If you have a sedan, you might need to carry your child's potty chair in the trunk and take it into a public rest room for your child to pee or poop.

Hauling around the potty chair or adapter won't last forever. This strategy is best for the more rigid child, who needs absolute consistency. For most families and children, bringing a potty out and about with you is too much of a hassle and just plain unrealistic. If you need to go back to Pull-Ups for errands and unexpected activities, you probably won't sabotage the whole toilet training effort. On the other hand, finding a time to focus on toilet training without such disruptions is ideal.

The Potty Copycat

Despite all the time and expense you put into buying a potty chair or toilet adapter seat, your child may insist on sitting on the toilet just as you do. Children are copycats and some feel that they're accomplishing the toileting task when they sit right on the big toilet. If this is the method your child chooses, then it's up to you to kneel on the floor next to the toilet to make sure your child doesn't fall in.

If your child is one who really wants to sit on the big toilet, it's even more important to have a step stool so he can step up to the toilet on his own. The stool serves as a secure place to set his feet and use as leverage when pushing out a poop.

Laying Out Your Expectations

When you buy the potty chair or seat, make it clear to your toddler that you expect she'll learn to use the toilet. Be encouraging and proud of your child as she takes small steps toward learning to use the toilet.

For some children, using the term "big boy" or "big girl" with accomplishments on the toilet can add pressure. Many children have ambivalent feelings about being a big kid. Some days, they want to dress themselves, play independently, and go to sleep without you in the room. Other days they're more needy, clingy, and babyish. Children go back and forth between meeting the challenges of growing up and wishing to remain a baby.

This might be the case if there's a new baby in the house. A child may come right out and say, "I don't want to be a big kid. I want to wear diapers just like baby Jack."

Respond with support but clear intentions: "Sometimes you still want to be a baby, I understand; nevertheless, you still need to learn to use the toilet."

When your child has any success toward toilet training, it's best to describe precisely what the child did and offer congratulations: "You sat on the toilet and tried to make a pee-pee. Good for you!"

In many respects when it comes to inspiring your child to want to use the toilet, you walk a fine line.

On the one hand, you want your child to know that you expect him to learn to sleep through the night in his own bed. You expect him to eat at the table with the family, dress himself, and put toys away. You also expect that he will learn to use the toilet. It's what people do in our world. On the other hand, you must honor your child, and your child alone controls the process. It's his body. In fact, there are few things he controls: what he eats, when he sleeps, and when he poops or pees. Parents can keep children in the bedroom or crib, make them sit at the table, and make them sit on the toilet; the body functions themselves are up to the child. When he learns to use the potty is up to him, but make it clear that all people, in their own way and time, go in the toilet.

And now, because he's growing up, his body is bigger and stronger and smarter, so it's time for him to start to learn. If you don't introduce the prospect of using the toilet, how will your child know what you expect?

When you communicate to your child your expectations, resist saying in a sugary-sweet, childish voice something like, "Sweetie, mommy really wants you to use the toilet. It would make her so happy." Trying to convince him to use the toilet out of his sense of obligation to you could backfire. He's too smart; he knows you're just trying to get him to do something he does not want to do. This won't work, and it won't get your child more interested or motivated to be toilet trained.

You also need to avoid yelling hysterically or even commanding your child with, "You go in that bathroom and pee right now because I said so! I know you know how and are just being a bad little boy!" Again, forcing your child to do this isn't going to work. Remember, you can make him go into the bathroom but you can't make him go in the toilet.

If you have fallen into one of those patterns, you aren't alone. Many parents become so frustrated that they resort to extreme behavior, hoping it will help the child learn the skill. Try to remember these strategies:

- Send a clear message.
- Don't add pressure.
- Build on the skills your child already has.

So instead, with a clear voice and strong body language, make your point. Say, "One day, when you feel the pee is ready to come out, you'll walk in the bathroom, pull down your pants, and go in the toilet." This is a direct message, no guilt or pressure, and shows your child that you believe in her and know she will be ready.

Potty Do's

Practice is a critical step on the road to potty training.

Encouraging Practice

Once you have purchased the potty chair, it's time to have your child sit on it to become comfortable. The child can be fully dressed, and later, can sit while wearing a diaper, disposable training pant, or cloth training pant. As this practice continues, encourage your child to sit on the potty chair and practice with a bare bottom.

Remember not to say, "Do you need to go potty?" A toddler might instinctively say "No!" just to prove her independence. Therefore, it's more effective and even inspiring for you to say, "Come on, it's time to sit on the potty. I need to sit on the big potty; you can practice peeing and pooping on the little potty with me."

Escort your child into bathroom. While you can't force a child to perform on the toilet, you can do your best to give him the opportunity to practice. Just as you sit your child in his high chair three to five times a day to eat, sit your child on the potty chair two to three times a day to practice using it.

Children don't always eat at every meal when they're toddlers, and toddlers don't always perform on the toilet every time they sit on the potty. But in time, the child will come to the table to eat and will go into the bathroom to pee and poop. How will they learn either without practice?

Potty Don'ts _____

Never force your child to sit on the toilet. You can be a bit insistent and you can always offer encouragement. You can, say to the reluctant child, "Well you didn't want to sit on the potty but you stood next to it and looked at it—someday you'll sit there."

How long your child practices before performing is up to him. The purpose of these practice sessions is to make your child feel comfortable and familiar with sitting on the potty chair. When that's done, performance will follow. Ideally, during one of the practice sessions, a pee or poop will come out. This may be your child's first success, and a high five or big hug should follow. Be careful though, and re-iterate that these are still practice sits, that making a pee or a poop isn't necessary.

Boy and Girl Strategies

While boys and girls are certainly made differently, when it comes to learning to use the toilet, both boys and girls can be either eager and willing or hesitant and reluctant. Regardless of gender, each individual child will have his or her own approach to learning to use the toilet. Some will have little interest in the process, while others will sit on the potty for long periods and do nothing. Each child is different and unique.

Parents often ask if they should teach their boys to sit or stand to pee. There is no right way. It's up to you, the teacher. Most potty chairs come with a shield to keep the urine from spraying on the floor. If your child uses such a shield, you need to keep an eye out so your son doesn't injure himself with it. You can also teach your son to push his penis pointing down to make sure the urine goes directly into the potty or toilet.

If you teach your son to sit for urinating, don't worry—in time, when he's at preschool, childcare, or school, he'll stand at the urinal with the other boys. Some boys, taking their instructions from Dad, stand to pee from the start. If your son does so, make sure you teach him to raise the lid on the toilet, aim into the water, flush, and then put the toilet seat back down; he can put the seat down before flushing, too. Some parents teach their boys to climb on the big toilet sitting backward. They can pee sitting down to start and then eventually from this position easily stand to pee.

To improve aim, families have been known to paint targets on the bottom of the toilet. Boys and their fathers can compete to see who has the best aim.

Another trick is to put blue food coloring in the toilet bowl. When yellow urine is added, the water turns green. Be warned: food coloring may stain your toilet bowl permanently.

Girls sit for both peeing and pooping so their task is a bit easier. You must instruct your daughter, however, to wipe herself after urinating. It's important to teach her to wipe thoroughly from front to

back (to prevent bringing germs from the rectum
to the vagina). Tell your little girl to "pat, pat, pat"
rather than wiping hard. This helps to eliminate
possible irritation or rashes.

Using Role Models

Once toddlers show regular interest in their family's bathroom activities, it's helpful to allow your
toddler to watch you or older siblings when they
go to the bathroom.

Training Trivia

Seeing grown-ups or siblings use the toilet often makes toddlers want to do the
same.

Fathers and grandfathers should show the correct
toilet skills to little boys, and mothers and grand-
mothers to little girls. Children can learn these
skills from older brothers and sisters, too.

If she's your only child, she may learn best in a daycare or preschool setting. The group may line up
to use the bathroom, and she will see that her peers
all use the toilet. A child may not be inspired by
Mom and Dad; after all, they're grown-ups and can
do most activities—drive a car, use the lawn mower,
and cut with sharp knives—that children can't.

Girls typically are ready to start potty training before boys of the same age. And boys can sometimes take longer to train than girls. Why? Perhaps because moms are usually the ones overseeing and modeling toileting procedures. The message to dads is to get involved in teaching your son to use the toilet. Toileting is a bit more complicated for boys because they must learn to sit to poop and stand to pee. That's why boys need their dads to be their toileting role model.

Using Toys to "Pretend"

Using a toy as pretend play is another way for your child to get excited about using the toilet. It's an alternative or additional method for your child to learn about toileting. Just like watching parents or siblings use the toilet, this planned play reassures your reluctant child that using the potty is a normal activity, and shows them it can be fun.

Play is a good thing for the child who is ready to begin potty training. As part of the daily play, encourage your child to take a teddy bear or doll to pee or poop on the toilet.

With the child's imagination in full force, seeing a doll or teddy use the potty is often enough to ease the child's way. If your child has a play area that includes a doll bed, kitchen set, table, or dolly high chair, include the potty chair before it begins real use.

Through their daily play activity, children will warm up to the idea of using the toilet themselves. They also may have the opportunity to work out their fears about using the toilet through play. Join in their play by announcing it's time for the teddy or doll to use the potty.

Accidents Will Happen

As the potty training commences, expect accidents. They are going to happen. It's part of the process.

Always look for interest from your child in using the potty while training. You can always encourage the interest, too. When your child is first showing interest in potty training, or after an accident, set your child on the toilet or potty-chair after cleaning her up.

"I just changed your diaper, someday you'll sit on the potty to pee and poop." With this method your child gets the idea that pee and poop go in the toilet.

Encouragement will go a long way to help potty train a reluctant child. Try to compliment every toileting step your child makes, including hand washing. Your child will eventually progress from practice doing each of the pieces of potty training to performing the whole thing.

Potty Don'ts _____

If you don't notice and talk about your child's small steps toward learning to use the toilet, she may not know how well she's doing and then decide not to bother.

Downplaying Setbacks

Before you start toilet training, think about how you will handle your child's accidents. Remember, we are working on inspiring the child to want to be trained, so failures have to be minimized. Now is the time to be prepared, as accidents will happen. For example, take extra clothes in the car and be prepared for wash-ups and clothing changes.

Deal with accidents as matter-of-factly as possible. If you respond to an accident with a lengthy discussion, loud voice, upset face, and heavy-duty disappointment, you may make the accident a bigger deal than it is. Your child might respond by feeling overwhelmed by the whole thing. If he were an adult, he might realize he can avoid your response simply by using the toilet next time. Unfortunately, he's 2 or 3 years old!

He's more likely to respond by trying to completely ignore the toileting thing to avoid this problem again. Also, even your negative attention is attention. Your child may enjoy all that time with you, even if you were yelling, and learn that having accidents gets parental attention, making him want to have accidents!

So, be matter of fact when accidents occur. Don't have elaborate conversations and explanations. Simply clean up the child and indicate that when ready, the child will have all the pees and poops in the toilet.

Avoid Negative Associations

Just as you want your child to feel comfortable about the need to sleep and eat, you want your child to feel just fine about the need to use the toilet. Sure, poop can be icky and smelly, but everyone makes them, and everyone must learn to manage his or her own bathroom responsibilities.

When talking about potty activities to your child, avoid using words like "stinky," "bad," "gross," or "dirty" to describe your child's waste. Use of these kinds of negative terms could make your child feel self-conscious or ashamed. It's always best for you and family members to handle urination and bowel movements in a simple, straightforward, and matter-of-fact manner.

When you toilet train your child, you're focusing on one of the most personal and private parts of your child's body. Approach this important task with both dignity and respect. You may need to be aware of your own facial expressions and the tone of your voice. Your child will notice them, even if you don't.

Potty Don'ts _____

Shame and disgust have no part in the potty training process.

Deciding What Words to Use

Before beginning potty training, you should carefully decide the words you and your family will use during the process. Carefully choose words that appropriately describe body parts and that are anatomically correct. You also need to use words that others outside your immediate family will understand.

If your child is playing at a friend's home, you want your child to use a word the parents will understand. If your child attends childcare or for some unforeseen reason is hospitalized, your child will need a word that will correctly communicate the need to use the toilet. Urine, pee, and pee-pee, and bowel movement, BM, poop, poo, doody, and caca are commonly used in the English language.

Training Trivia _____

Remember that many others—friends, neighbors, teachers, clergy, relatives, and other caregivers—will also hear these words. It's always best to use words that won't offend, confuse, or embarrass your child, you, or others.

Remember that your child is absorbing everything you say. If you call a bowel movement "poop," so will your child. If you call it something else that might be offensive to others, you'd better change your ways. No one will be offended by the words pee or poop.

In time, as your child matures, you'll offer a more refined way to announce the need to go, such as, "Excuse me, may I use your bathroom?" For now, when your child announces the need to pee or poop, you'll need to shed your embarrassment. Just be glad your child is communicating about the need to go, can wait until he gets into the bathroom, and is willing to do so.

Choose your words carefully!

The Least You Need to Know

- Familiarize your child with the bathroom and make it a task that is appealing.
- Allow your child to choose between a potty chair or toilet seat adapter.
- Use role models and pretend with toys to help encourage training.
- Downplay accidents and setbacks; avoid negative associations with bathroom responsibilities.
- Decide what words to use before beginning training and choose your words carefully.

Dealing with Preschool Deadlines

In This Chapter

- Potty training for preschool
- Establishing a regular routine
- Working with daycare and preschool teachers
- Dealing with unsolicited advice

One of the problems with life—and potty training—is there are so many schedules we need to keep. We live by them. Your employer expects you to be at your job at your start time. You see a doctor or dentist by appointment. Stores open and close at specific times.

You're likely to feel the pressure to get your son or daughter trained because of a deadline, or someone else's schedule. It could be that you must return to work, and daycare or preschool pressures are setting a specific date on a calendar. In other words, your child must be trained by a specific date.

While your world is on one schedule, your child may be on a very different one. Fear not! This chapter covers some of the things you can do to help try to meet your on-time training goals.

Getting Trained Before Preschool

Many preschools require that children be potty trained before entering their programs. In child-care centers, some children aren't allowed to move into a classroom for preschool-aged children until they're using the toilet by themselves.

Schools cite health concerns regarding wiping children. They may say that teachers aren't trained or don't have the time to change diapers. They may say that a child who isn't toilet trained isn't mature enough for their program. In fact, private schools can accept or refuse any child based on how well the school thinks the child will do there, and how well the school can provide for that child's needs.

Unfortunately, these requirements often present a problem. What's a parent to do?

Your first step is to relax. Then the next step is to stop relaxing, and get started. Reading this book is a great step toward getting started (if we do say so ourselves!). Here are some other considerations when on a tight schedule ….

Do your best to focus on training without distractions. Somehow try not to allow your child to pick up on the rushed time frame. It's your chance to be an award-winning actor.

Rather than working on each new task or skill for a week, shorten the schedule. Your toddler can pick up a new "job" every few days.

Think carefully about rewards. Go right for high yield motivators, such as special time with a parent. (There will be much more information about this in Chapter 7.)

Get your child on a preset schedule. Starting your child on the same schedule as his upcoming preschool can really help. Try matching the upcoming school day, for example, breakfast at 6:45 every day. In a short time, the schedule becomes routine, to you and your child. Now look at your child's toileting pattern, and put a sit-down time at the time he regularly goes. In other words, if your child usually poops after breakfast, then put in a regular sit-down time 20 to 30 minutes after the meal.

Some children don't go at a predictable time. Try this: give your child high-fiber foods such as fruit and cereals as midday snacks. This might get your child on a schedule of making a bowel movement in the evening. You can help that along by making the sit-down time after dinner. This could be when both the fiber and dinner will lead to a successful bowel movement.

Once your child regularly poops when the sun is down, you can honestly tell the teacher, "I know my child won't have a bowel movement at school, and if he does, I'll come to the school and change him."

Potty Do's

Feeding fruits to your child is always a good snack. And they can help make it easier to start your child on a schedule of regular bowel movements.

As the day approaches when your child is scheduled to begin daycare or preschool, you may have a child who is almost toilet trained, just not completely trained yet. Maybe your child uses the toilet sometimes, but ignores poops and pees when playing or watching TV.

Tell the teacher about the child's potty progress, and ask, "Can my child begin preschool and see how it goes? I believe that my child will watch the other children and in no time always use the toilet with them." It's all in the presentation!

Sometimes, your child might do well at the preschool, and even use the toilet better than at home. Your child may feel little or no pressure at preschool or daycare to use the potty, even if going at home is very stressful. At school, toileting may be merely part of the daily routine and not experienced as a specific individual task. Your child may go to the bathroom when all the other children go. Not being singled out could remove any pressure of performance.

Your child might be one who will do things for his teacher that he won't do for you. As frustrating as that may be, some kids know which buttons they can push with their moms or dads. It's called their personalities. Remember, they get them from you!

Potty Do's _____

Don't be surprised at the influence from the other kids at preschool. Copying what the other kids (or even better yet, the older kids) are doing is a terrific incentive for your child. It will work much better than subtle parental pressure.

What If It Can't Be Done?

While they want their child in a preschool program, or in the room at the childcare center with same-aged friends, parents' hands are sometimes tied. If the child refuses to use the toilet, or just isn't ready, or isn't interested, the preschool you were planning on may not be possible.

If you can't complete training in time for the first day of school, work with the teacher. Ask, "Can I send my child to school in disposable training pants?"

Talking with the preschool teacher can often lead to solutions. The teacher might be able to shed some light on the problem. Learn about the school's schedule, and what they say and do with the children.

Whatever you decide to do, don't pressure your child by saying, "In two months, preschool starts. You've just got to learn to use the toilet or you can't go."

Although this information is correct, it will likely not motivate your child to use the toilet. Your child has no idea just when two months is, and he does not know what to do to learn to use the toilet. More likely, he will see how pressured you feel, and respond with even more reluctance.

Potty Don'ts

Pressuring your child, because of time, to use the toilet never works.

Unsolicited Advice

Unfortunately, some grandparents might notice the daycare requirement and choose to share their own training opinions with you. Members of the older generations—grandparents and great-grandparents—often state that potty training should begin much earlier. The older generation may declare their children were trained between 12 and 18 months.

Those were the good old days of potty training when the parent was in charge of the process. The parent would sit the child on the toilet when seeing the signs that he was about "to go" and catch the poop or pee at the right time. With a certain cry, backstretch, facial grimace, or gas sound, parents can sometimes recognize the child is about to have a bowel movement or urination, and hold the child over the toilet. It was the parent's accomplishment.

Training Trivia

Chinese babies often wear split bottom pants so they can squat to make a poop easily. Infants in India, Kenya, and Greenland are often trained before one year of age.

In the United States up to the 1940s parents were advised to hold the baby over the toilet. With the advent of washing machines and then cheaper and disposable diapers, parents were advised to train the child at an older age and have him wear diapers until he was ready to toilet independently. Today, most kids train when they're between 2 and 3 years old.

In fact, some parents today still start children training with this method. Particularly in countries where infants spend the day strapped to their mothers, such early toileting is common.

In the United States, a smaller portion of parents choose this method. Toileting at such a young age isn't impossible, but it's not the child who is trained. Yes, the poops and pees may go into the toilet, but the child isn't independent. The child isn't necessarily recognizing the feeling of having to go, and isn't holding it in until reaching the bathroom.

It's actually the parent who is trained and not the child. These parents are trained to read the child's signals, and then get the child to the bathroom. This method may work in infants, before the independence of toddler-hood takes over. An infant held over a potty will let loose, while a toddler may well fight back. Don't try holding your 2½-year-old over the toilet to make a pee or poop—the consequences will surely be disastrous!

Parenting has changed over the years. For better or for worse, we follow the child's lead. We introduce new opportunities, like different foods, games, and clothes. We encourage the child to at least try, but if there is no interest we tend not to push. Toilet training nowadays is similar. The common approach is to see if the child has the skills and interest needed for training, then we help them along but make toileting the child's independent task in his toddler years.

When your mother or grandmother offers her advice, thank her for it, and then do what feels right for your family and in the best interest of your child.

One grandparent suggested that his grandson should be trained with the naked $100 method. It's simple: allow the child to run around the house naked. As the pees and poops naturally occur, the child will dislike it enough to start using the potty. The $100 is used for supplies to clean the carpet. The $100 "reward" is for the parents, not the child! This method may work, but the reluctant child probably needs much more support.

Remember, the age a child uses the bathroom alone varies. It's based only on a child's readiness to be trained and the positive attitude of the parents. Some children may postpone having a bowel movement as a way to manipulate their parents or because they're busy doing something else. Try not to make an issue of this.

The important thing to remember is that potty training is on your child's schedule, not yours or the preschool's. You need to begin your routine, work toward the goal of training, and hope it works out in time. If it doesn't, it doesn't. You will need to delay the preschool attendance or switch schools. If that happens, it happens. It's up to your child. While you can encourage potty training, you can't make it happen by a specific date.

The Least You Need to Know

- Don't stress out over the date preschool starts; try to get your child on his preschool's schedule in advance, and stick to it.

- Work with daycare and preschool teachers to aid in your potty training efforts.
- Potty training is on your child's schedule, not yours or the preschool's.

Chapter 5

Getting Ready to Start

In This Chapter

- Organizing in advance
- Getting your approach, attitude, and clothes in check
- Going from training pants to underwear

It's time to get ready to begin the potty training. As the day approaches, you need to get prepared. From a supply of clean underwear to timing, there are lots of things to consider and plan. This chapter will get you prepared and ready to do battle with the potty poopers.

Getting Organized

You must get everything ready for the big start day. It's not as overwhelming as you might first think. It's just a matter of preplanning and organizing early.

Get all of your supplies ready. Your list should include:

❏ Clean underwear

❏ The potty, toilet seat cover, or traveling potty

❏ Rewards

❏ Appropriate clothing for your toddler (easy to slide on and off)

❏ An optimistic attitude

Planning the Start

Timing is everything when it comes to potty training. You want to have long, uninterrupted periods. One great option is when older children are away at camp. Try not to start at other times when daily activities might be interrupted. For example, during the holidays isn't a good time to begin. There will just be too many interruptions to your daily schedule, even with your best efforts.

You should also try not to have other major stresses in your life. That's probably easier said than done, but as much as you can, try to reduce other activities and interactions that strain your attitude and drain your energy.

Avoid times when your child is going through a bad phase. The terrible twos have these times. It's part of every toddler's life. I'm sure you know what I am talking about here.

It's also best to plan the start when your child isn't experiencing other major changes, such as a new teacher, new baby-sitter, or new baby in the family.

Recognizing the Age to Begin

There is no preset, specific age for when to begin potty training. The right time is when a child has developed …

- physically (his bowel and bladder control).
- intellectually (he knows in his mind that his bowel or bladder is full and can communicate about it).
- socially (he realizes that others use the toilet).
- emotionally (he is willing to give up diapers and go in the toilet).

When your child has matured in all these areas, then it's time to begin potty training, even if your child appears reluctant.

It's a myth that all toddlers want to give up their beloved diapers. It's all they've known from birth. Many enjoy diaper-changing time when you and your toddler interact, play, and sing.

If you want your child to learn to use the toilet, be sure to alter your routine to give a lot of attention when he's on his little potty and little attention when you're changing diapers.

Potty Do's _____

As you make the transition from diapers to underwear, use your attention wisely. Focus off the child when diapering and on him when toileting.

Two less obvious indicators that your child is ready to learn to use the toilet:

Indicator 1. Your child knows where various household items belong. The pots and pans go in the cupboard, coats and boots go in this closet, paper and pencils go in that drawer. Believe it or not, this is one sign that your child is ready to learn to use the toilet. If children know where various household items go, they can understand that pee and poop should be put where they belong, which is in the toilet!

Indicator 2. Your child imitates your behavior. If you see your toddler trying to comb her hair, put on make-up, use shaving cream, read the newspaper, or use your cell phone, these copycat behaviors indicate that she's ready to copy what you do in the bathroom.

Remember there is no specific date that you must begin (or complete) potty training. It's more of a range of ages. Don't pressure yourself or your child by pushing to have the training started or completed by a certain age of the child.

Training Trivia

A good sign to begin potty training is when the child shows interest in adults' use of the toilet.

Consider Your Approach and Attitude

Stay upbeat and positive. Communicate that you expect your child will learn to use the toilet but that he and he alone is in control of his body. Some days you'll be frustrated, and won't be able to stop yourself from communicating your frustrations.

When you do this, be careful not to harm the process by being too angry or emotional. If you must share, try to be neutral and speak with as few words as possible: "I'm frustrated, I see you peeing on the carpet and you're able to pee in the toilet. Next time I know you can go in the toilet."

Get yourself ready to be patient with your child and the potty training process. There are going to be trying times. You will have your child on the potty for 10 minutes, with no results, and 5 minutes later, while playing, your child will go. It happens. While you don't remember it, you did the same thing. Be patient!

For a successful potty training experience, both parents must be on board. Parents have to be supportive of each other, and agree about the process. Both have to stop what they're doing whenever the child needs their help or assistance. The temporary inconvenience must occur for the training to be successful.

Ready, Set, Dress!

Before beginning the actual training, one other consideration is to make sure that your child's wardrobe is adaptable to potty training. It's time to change the daily clothing that your child has been wearing.

Eliminate clothes from your child's wardrobe that include belts, buckles, buttons, zippers, and snaps. Simple clothes are now necessary. Your child must be able to undress by herself without any assistance. Eliminate the following kinds of clothing during the potty training process:

- Clothing with fasteners
- Snowsuits
- One-piece outfits for sleep (footy pajamas)
- Overalls
- Leotards

Little girls can wear dresses or skirts. Boys and girls can wear sweat pants or elastic-waist shorts.

The easier it is for your child to get clothes up and down, the more willing and skillful your child will be when using the toilet. Also, once your child begins using the toilet, feeling the need to go may come instantly. When they realize they have to go, they may have little time before going. So, the easier you can make the clothing go on and off, the less time it'll take for your little one to make it to the toilet.

Potty Do's

Independence is a big aspect for the reluctant child to learn to use the toilet. The easier the child's clothing is to manage, the more independent your child can and will be.

Switching from Diapers to Pants

Another consideration is disposable training pants (Pull-Ups) versus cotton training pants versus underwear. There are some things to consider and keep in mind:

- Disposable training pants are convenient and useful when first starting out.
- Cotton training pants have an extra layer or two of material designed to absorb urine.
- Underwear does not have the extra layer of material, so the child will feel the urine faster.

Each item—disposable training pants, cotton training pants, and lightweight cotton underwear—has its advantages and disadvantages. You have to decide when it's appropriate to use each with your child.

Disposable Training Pants/Pull-Ups

Use Pull-Ups before you start training. Accidents are absorbed in Pull-Ups, so children can wear them before they're trained to use the toilet. However, your child can pull them down easily and have the chance to practice this necessary step before starting the full-fledged training process.

Pull-Ups (or disposable training pants) are also great to use during the training process for naps, nighttime, travel, or anytime when away from home. During the day, some children learn quickly that they're just like a diaper. Then they might start using their Pull-Ups just as a diaper, peeing and pooping in them. Your child may not mind if they soiled the Pull-Ups because they're actually as absorbent as a diaper. This dryness may not help to motivate your child to use the potty.

Pull-Ups are good in the beginning of training when your child is showing interest but has not yet developed consistency. They work well when the child is running to the bathroom frequently. Pull-Ups go up and down like underwear, which you'll appreciate as much as your child, since diaper tabs begin to wear out after a short while.

One positive thing about Pull-Ups is that they're different from diapers. Your child will feel more grown-up. Once your child starts using the Pull-Ups (pulling them down and up), moving him to cotton training pants or underwear is the next step.

Cotton Training Pants

Cotton training pants, with their extra layer of material to absorb urine, help your child realize they're no longer in diapers. Don't be too surprised that you still find puddles of pee on the floor after an accident. While the training pants are designed to absorb more, they won't absorb everything. Some parents move their children to training pants before taking the plunge into underwear. For children who are still having accidents in their Pull-Ups, training pants are a good intermediate step.

Underwear

Regular underwear does not have the extra padding or layers of material found in training pants. Cleaning up after an accident will take longer. You can put a rubber pant on over the underwear or you can put on disposable training pants to avoid messes on carpets, floors, and sofas.

Your child will realize quickly when the underwear is wet or soiled. This can help to encourage the use of the potty.

Potty Do's

Your child might become discouraged or humiliated if there are too many accidents in her underwear. Therefore, it's always a good idea for your child to have had some successes on the toilet before they start wearing underwear.

Another option is to have her wear underwear for brief periods of time when she'll likely stay clean. For example, after a poop or a pee, clean her up and practice wearing undies for an hour. Put her back in diapers or training pants afterward, and celebrate the successful dry time she had. See Chapter 6 for more details about starting underwear.

Wearing underwear has many benefits:

- It allows the child to feel wetness or a stool.
- It makes the child feel more grown up.
- It's part of the fun of learning something new.

Potty Don'ts

Change your child's soiled underwear or training pants quickly. You don't want your child to get used to the feeling of soiled underwear or training pants. You want the most familiar feeling to be clean and dry.

A Breakthrough Example

An almost 3-year-old toddler was reluctant to use the toilet. He had been in Pull-Ups since he turned 2½ years old and liked them.

Even though his mother had purchased Spiderman underwear, he refused to wear them. He wanted them pulled on over his Pull-Ups. He would sit on the toilet before getting in the bathtub but he had never gone.

The toddler had a little potty chair that sat on the floor but he refused to use it—he wanted to sit on the big toilet like his older brother and sister. One day, unfortunately, when sitting on the toilet he slipped, and his bottom fell into the toilet with a splash. Needless to say, this experience scared him and set him back even further, and now he refused to even practice on the toilet.

Mom thought of another tactic. She announced one day in a forthright fashion, "There's a rule in our house now that says when you're home you wear underwear!" There was no direct pressure to use the toilet, so the child didn't refuse. The child loved his Spiderman underwear, so was glad for the new rule. His fear of the toilet made it a hard decision for him. His desire to wear his special underwear made it easier to accept this plan that included his potty training.

Mom dressed him in his underwear, and all was well and good. That evening as Mom prepared dinner, he stood on a chair that was pushed up to the kitchen table. He was working on a puzzle when all of a sudden he peed. The toddler gasped as he felt the pee run down his leg and onto the chair. He wasn't happy that he got Spidee all wet.

It was the first time he put together that he could stop the pee from coming out to keep himself dry. Mom didn't overreact with exasperation. She simply carried him into the bathroom, cleaned him up and sat him on the toilet and spoke in calm and reassuring tones.

"Pee goes in the toilet. The next time you feel the need to pee, tell Mommy and I'll bring you in the bathroom; I won't let you fall in the toilet and we'll keep those underwear dry!"

Although the boy had a few more accidents, this episode was a breakthrough event that helped him on the road to learning to use the toilet.

The Least You Need to Know

- Plan the start of potty training by getting everything organized.
- Communicate positively that you expect your child to learn to use the toilet, but that he and he alone is in control of his body.
- Dress your child with easy-off clothing.
- Pull-Ups, cotton training pants, and light-weight cotton underwear all have their advantages and disadvantages when beginning potty training.

Chapter 6

Let the Training Begin!

In This Chapter

- Starting the training
- Knowing what's working and what's not
- Dealing with frustration (yours and your child's!)

You've read half of this book, and are probably still wondering how to start the training process. You've laid the groundwork and want to get that kid trained already! In this chapter, you'll learn exactly what to do. But, if you're anything like us, you might have skipped right to this chapter, eager to get to the real meat. A word to the wise: jumping right into toilet training the reluctant child could well fail, if it hasn't already. It's worth taking the time to understand why your child is reluctant, and what you as a parent can do to avoid power struggles. Then you can get your child excited about training, and have all the paraphernalia you'll need to make all of your efforts a success.

So if you jumped ahead, consider starting from the beginning and then you will be more ready to tackle this chapter on how to start potty training your child.

The Day You Begin

The day you begin has finally arrived. You're ready! You've removed the stress and pressure that were getting in the way. You've made the bathroom ready and gotten your child interested. You know what your child can and can't do, and you know which skills to work on first. Take a deep breath, put a real smile on, and face that resistant child. You know you can help him meet this milestone.

Making the Plan

Maybe you have already introduced potty training with small steps, as outlined in Chapter 5. You're reading this book because it didn't work. Just a little more prepwork could be the difference between success and failure.

Two Hours a Day in Underwear

For starters, maybe your child needs a little more motivation and success to make toileting progress. Before you start your step-by-step plan, put dry underwear into the mix. After your child urinates, clean her up and put her in underwear. Tell her that it's practice, for her to feel big-girl panties.

This is where those special cartoon character, superhero-themed fashion statements come in. The trick is, however, to make it a surefire success. How do you do this? Limit the time she wears the undies to maximize her chance of staying dry. If you put them on after changing a wet diaper or Pull-Ups, her bladder should be empty when you put the underwear on. She won't have to go for another 2 to 3 hours. This is your window of dryness. Start with brief trials: after 30 minutes change her back into diapers or Pull-Ups, and cheer the dryness. After a few days or a week, extend the underwear time, until you reach 2 hours. Be sure she knows what a good job she did in keeping the pee-pee out of those underwear.

Some parents get greedy here; they become excessively optimistic. They extend the underwear time too long, and an accident is unavoidable. It is so tempting to leave that underwear on longer in hopes the end has come. Don't fall into this trap. Leaving underwear on for too long will most likely lead to messy accidents, ruining the opportunity for your child's success. During some trials there will be accidents; stay neutral and upbeat. If your child wets after 20 minutes, decrease the trial time to 15 minutes so she feels successful, and then slowly make the trials longer and longer.

For the few weeks before you start your toilet training steps, your child will be spending two hours a day in underwear. This might motivate her to want to be trained, when she can wear underwear all day and have even more success. At the same time, she may be learning how to "hold it in," in her effort to stay dry.

Count the days down to her by crossing them off on a calendar. Build the excitement in a positive and exciting manner by highlighting the start date, but be sure you are encouraging without pressuring. Choose your words carefully. Be reassuring, and use words that your child can say to herself when she starts to feel less sure. Tell her, "Just say, 'I can do it.'" Read books every night at bedtime about toileting, so your child experiences toileting success through the characters in the stories.

Determine the best 2-hour period each day when you will be home and you can dress your child in underwear. It will be best if the time frame is the same each day.

For example, from 8 A.M. to 10 A.M., after a diaper change, might work best for stay-at-home moms. Or the 6 P.M. to 8 P.M. period, after the post-dinner pee-pee, might fit better for parents who work outside of the home.

Your daily schedule might not be so fixed. Perhaps your lifestyle requires you to juggle a changing schedule, and you cannot find a consistent 2-hour period each day. If so, don't allow that to stop the potty training. You'll just need to be sure to schedule the 2-hour period each day. Although not the preferred option, you can make this work. One day, for example, the 2-hour period might fall between 10 A.M. and noon, and the following day it might be between 4 P.M. and 6 P.M. Just be sure to put on

underwear after a diaper change when your child's
bladder is empty.

Potty Do's

It's important to schedule the 2-hour sessions, start them, and stick with them.

A Week Prior to Your Start Date

A week before your start date, organize your life
and home to prepare for the training to start. Have
the potty chair sitting in the bathroom, all ready
for when your child is ready. Hang some stickers
from the fridge, tantalizing your child. When he
asks what they're for, tell him the stickers are for
some jobs he can do. Tell him you're going to start
practicing, so he can use the toilet when he's ready.
Tell him you have super special sparkly stickers for
him, too.

Now's the time to get groceries, pay bills, make
play dates for your other kids. Be sure your child's
easy-access clothes are clean and ready. If your
child is in daycare, talk to the teacher. Tell him or
her what you are doing at home, and figure out
how it can be consistent there, too. Expect that
with the demand of training, your child's behavior
at school might be affected, and ask the teacher to
keep in touch with you.

A Step-by-Step Place to Start

You've done much work to get to this point. The fighting with your child, spouse, and in-laws about toilet training is gone, and so you're biting your tongue all the time. You've made the bathroom the world's most enticing room to a child: sports and entertainment magazines are gone, with potty books, talking toys, and fuzzy stuffed animals in their place. You are the proud owner of a potty, chosen—and perhaps decorated—with the excellent taste of your toddler. Even your child looks different, wearing only elastic waist pants and skirts that provide easy access. You've cleared your schedule, hoping to do it finally! You're ready, and so is your child.

So, how do you start? Well, let's go back to the list of steps that every kid has to do to be toilet trained. It helps to check off which skills your child can already do and which are jobs still to learn.

Does your child …

- ❑ feel it coming?
- ❑ hold it in?
- ❑ communicate the need to go?
- ❑ get to the toilet?
- ❑ pull down pants, underpants?
- ❑ sit on the toilet?
- ❑ relax?
- ❑ make a poop or pee?

- ❏ wipe?
- ❏ get off the toilet?
- ❏ pull up pants, underpants?
- ❏ flush?
- ❏ wash hands?

Parents sometimes aren't sure which of these steps a child can or can't do. Here are some hints.

"Feeling it coming" and "holding it in": If your child makes a poop in diapers or Pull-Ups while hiding under the dining room table or in the corner of the bedroom, then he feels it coming. After all, he has to feel it coming and hold it in so he can get to his special, private place. Sometimes parents can tell the child is feeling it from tense facial expressions or because the child stops what he's doing and just freezes in place.

"Communicate the need to go": Kids let their parents know they need to go in different ways. Some point to their diapers, and some use the words "I gotta go!" Some parents can see the child has to go by a certain expression on their child's face—usually a combination of surprise, fear, and confusion.

"Get to the toilet," "pulling down pants, underpants": These are motor skills that most parents can see their child doing. If you're not sure whether your child can do these or not, just give it a try. Tell your child that you're just practicing undressing and sitting—that you aren't asking her to make a poop or pee on the toilet. If she can't pull down her pants, try different waistbands, and be sure to avoid more complicated buttons and zippers. (For more information, see Chapter 5.)

"Sit on the toilet" and "relax": You've already started to take care of this, by buying a potty chair that's comfortable to your child with any foot support that's necessary, and by making the bathroom a fun, happy, stress-free place to be. If you haven't, then go back and read this book from the beginning. The question now is whether or not your child is comfortable on the potty or toilet. Does she sit while you are going? When she sits, is she loose like a goose or a bundle of nerves? Does she enjoy herself when sitting or is she desperate to get off that potty?

"Make a poop or pee": Obviously, your child isn't yet making poop or pee on the toilet—if he could do it, he would already be trained! However, pooping and peeing do have to be comfortable and regular. Kids who have pain with either pooping or peeing won't want to go, and will hold it in at all costs. If it hurts to go, skip ahead to Chapter 8 and read about constipation and other possible medical issues.

"Wipe": Most kids don't wipe well as toddlers. Their coordination and attention aren't the best, and they know their parents are going to clean them up anyway. That's fine. A child has to at least try the first wipe as part of the training process, even if mom finishes.

"Get off the toilet": Although this sounds like a simple task, some children are not steady enough to climb off the toilet. A small stool or step might make it easier for your child to do. Don't overlook simple solutions. What might appear to be a non-issue for you could be a big problem for your child, yet it could be easily solved.

"Pull up pants, underpants": Your child needs to be able to pull up their underpants and their pants. Getting everything back in place is the goal. Don't be surprised if at first your child is not perfectly tucking in his shirt. The goal here is to get the pants up. Neatness will follow in due time.

"Flush": Most children can master flushing. They might forget, or the handle on the toilet might need an adjustment, especially if it is difficult to move.

Potty Don'ts _____

Beware of your reaction to your child's poop. If you think it's gross, so will your child. Getting that child to wipe could become a real challenge.

"Wash hands": Independent training requires adequate hand washing. This means using warm water (not scalding hot) to scrub hands for about 15 seconds. You may need to observe how well your child really washes. As part of the hand washing process, you can teach your child to count to 10 or say a rhyme to help him gauge the right amount of time. Also, make sure your child dries her hands on a towel (which should be laundered at least weekly).

Hand washing is an important part of the toileting routine. Even if your child did not "go" in the potty, she needs to wash her hands. And always remember to wash your hands, too, setting a good example for your child.

Potty Do's

Antibacterial liquid foamy soap works best for washing hands.

Steps for Getting There

Getting your reluctant child to use the potty regularly requires methodic steps, combined with your patience and persistence. To assist you through the process, follow these steps.

Step One

Go through the checklist and figure out what your child can and can't do. If your child can't communicate the need to go or get to the toilet, he might not have the developmental skills to be independently trained. You can try teaching them, but most kids need to have the language and motor skills of at least the typical 2-year-old to be able to use the toilet independently.

Step Two

Now it's time to give your child a job to do. The goal is to have all the skills consolidated, so you are mostly working on the tasks your child can't do yet. Remember to give your child a choice. Tell her you know she's not ready to make on the toilet, so you're going to work on some other things. Pick two of the steps on the list, and ask her to pick which one should be her job. You can offer two jobs she can't do, or one she can and one she can't do. She might pick something she can already do, like flushing. That's okay. For a few days she practices flushing, and every time she does it, you praise her for doing such a good job. She starts to feel confident, and she picks a harder job next time.

For example, many kids are just stuck on the "sitting and relaxing" and "wiping" parts. In the first case, job number one might be to just sit on the toilet. Tell her it's just to get ready for when she wants to use the bathroom, that we're not using the toilet for poops and pees just yet.

If she gets uptight and stressed when she sits on the toilet (she's not relaxed), have her just practice sitting on the toilet, again with no expectation to produce. Tell her over and over that it's just practice—no pooping yet! Having her toys or books there will make it fun. If she's reluctant to sit, give her a new choice, without eliminating the sitting job. Tell her she can sit with the toilet seat up or down, or that she can sit with diapers on or off. Having a choice will make her feel more in control and less resistant.

If your child will not wipe, then wiping could be a job to choose. Your child might opt to use a disposable wipe, which will get the job done more easily than toilet paper but can still go down the toilet. Your child can start wiping before using the toilet. When you change the diaper or Pull-Ups, have the child take the first swipe and then you can finish the clean-up.

Each step that your child has not yet mastered can be rewarded as an individual job, separated out from the rest of the toileting sequence. Break the jobs down into the smallest piece necessary. Maybe your child will need to start with the second wipe, after you have cleaned up the "big stuff." Maybe you'll need to put your hand over your child's during that first wipe. Some kids may need to start by just ripping off the toilet paper and handing it over. Every step accomplished is a step in the right direction, an opportunity for successes as a base for more successes.

 Potty Do's

Giving children a choice will decrease their resistance by giving them some control. Be sure that all the choices you offer would be okay for the child to choose.

Whatever jobs your child chooses, communicate it specifically to all the other grown-ups involved in the training process. For example, if you opt to start with a practice sit-down time, then make sure everyone knows the goal isn't to produce. Remind your family that "you can't clench and make!" In other words, your bottom can't be all tightened for the poop to come out. Your child has to practice relaxing on the toilet, since that's a vital step in accomplishing toilet training.

Be sure to tell your spouse, relatives who care for your child, or your child's teacher what the job is. Anytime the job is done the child should be commended; this can be anything from a high five or a big hug to a small treat. See Chapter 7 for more ideas about incentives.

Step Three

Your child has already chosen his first job, let's say wiping or sitting. For a few days or weeks, he has practiced sitting every day or attempted the first wipe on several occasions, and was thrilled that you were thrilled or that he earned small treats. Now the successes are building—he's happy and so are you. Build on this trend. Tell him that he's doing great, and that now he doesn't need a reward for sitting or wiping anymore. It's time to pick a new job! Look back to the list of necessary skills for toilet training, and offer him another choice; maybe this time it's flushing or hand washing.

Step Four

Once your child has experienced some successes, it's time to add a regular sit-down time. This is to practice sitting, and not to make a poop or pee. The sit-down time can be a job that is rewarded, if your child hasn't already been doing it. If a sit-down time to practice relaxing has already become comfortable, then make a sit-down time part of the daily routine while other jobs are rewarded. Try to schedule these sit-down times about half an hour after meals, since the body has a natural reflex to go then. For the very reluctant child, be sure to offer the option of sitting fully clothed with the toilet seat down.

Remember Chapter 2? When we went on and on about having the time to do all of this without interruptions and stress? Now's the time it really matters. Since the goal is for your child to practice being relaxed on the toilet, he needs a stress-free time to do it. If you're tense, rushed, pulled in 17 directions, racing to leave the house for carpool, distracted by making dinner, helping with homework, cleaning the house, talking on the phone, paying bills—you get the idea—your child will pick up on your emotional state and will be anything but relaxed.

Step Five

Every few weeks, offer your child choices for a new job. Pick the skills on the list of tasks needed to potty train, until the only job left is to make a pee or poop on the toilet. Usually, when a child can do all the other steps, you'll see a confident child who feels happy and comfortable in the bathroom.

Potty Don'ts

Sit-down times are to practice being relaxed on the toilet. You can't expect the already-resistant child to "hurry up and poop."

Don't be surprised if you still have to suggest the last job, making into the toilet. Some kids need to go *really* slowly. They may have a job of pooping on the toilet, but with the toilet seat closed and with Pull-Ups on. Next, lift the seat. Some kids even need a final step of pooping with Pull-Ups on but with a hole cut out for the poop to go through!

Eventually, you will have to take away that layer of security. Some kids stick at this point for long periods, even wearing underwear all day and only asking for a diaper to make a poop or a pee into, while sitting on the toilet and wiping and washing independently. Use your judgment about when to remove the diaper option. Some kids are stuck at this stage for weeks or months. Sometimes the simple suggestion that there are no more diapers is enough to end their use or dependence on them.

Sensing Progress

So, you're in the middle of training your child, working on one job at a time. Maybe you've offered your child the choice to wipe or flush, to sit or wash hands. Some of these tasks he's done before, some he hasn't. Maybe you've gotten him to sit on the toilet a few times, but not nearly the three times per day we suggested in Chapter 3. It may be hard to get too excited about. Many kids will even have a single complete success in the early training period, and when you see that poop or pee in the bowl you think it's all over. Alas, the child returns to his reluctant little self. Try to see the bowl as half full, not half empty.

It may seem a tad tedious, but it helps if you jot down your child's daily elimination schedule. For instance:

- He wet in his disposable training pants in the morning.
- Put him in underwear at 9 A.M., still dry at 11 A.M.
- Put him back in disposable training pants at 11 A.M., had a bowel movement in them immediately.
- Happily did his sit-down time after lunch— he peed! He got a sticker on his chart.
- After his nap, Pull-Ups dry.
- Wore Pull-Ups the rest of the day, refused to do sit-down after dinner on schedule; given

the choice to sit after bath or before bath, chose before.

- Did his sit-down before taking his bath. Put another sticker on the chart.

By writing down how your child is doing, after a week you'll be able to determine your child's overall progress. Look for the new skills that may be hidden in your child's actions. The child described here peed in the toilet, but maybe that's not new. What is new might be he held in the poop until the Pull-Ups were on. Holding it in is a necessary step! He didn't agree to all of the sit-down times as scheduled, but he ended up doing it and enjoyed the rewards.

Watch yourself and your actions. Make sure you are not doing or saying anything that discourages the use of the toilet. Even the slightest sense of disappointment in your voice or on your face can be perceived as pressure.

Remember that you're orchestrating the learning process, but only to a point. While you need to get the ball rolling, at some point, your child will take the potty training reins. Look for when he does so.

Although you have a working plan, when you see that he's beginning to take control of the process, back off. Your goal is not that your child will learn to use the toilet when you tell him, but that he will take the responsibility for toileting away from you, and be in charge of the entire process himself.

Remember to support his interest when he shows signs of doing so.

A New Attitude

It's like the first time you take your child to the ocean or the lake. You've practiced paddling in the shallow pool, bought the floaties, and psyched your kid up for the fun at the beach. You get there, and the kid is a wreck and just puts a toe in the water, and then screeches and runs the other way. You know that all the skills are there, and so does the child, but he needs to test the water first; he's not quite ready to take the plunge. Eventually he'll dive right in, but until that time, there will be lots of toes, then ankles, then knees in the water. He's getting more and more of his body in each time. Toileting is the same, with small steps toward the end goal. Just being more willing to be in the bathroom or to sit on the toilet are signs that reluctance is dissolving.

Making Small Steps

Measure success by smaller steps than just a poop or pee in the toilet or lack thereof. The child might be more comfortable sitting, might be more willing to flush or wipe, even if it's not every single time. You might have some attempts to indicate the need to go, and the child might use the toilet once or twice at home or elsewhere. Go back to the checklist and see how many more items you are getting closer to checking off.

You might see less crying in response to the whole toileting process. Take a step back, and think about the fighting in your house about your child's untrained status. This change in attitude is progress. You've removed an obstacle getting in the way of your child's success.

Facing Tears and Tantrums

Let's face it, though, this is not going to be smooth sailing the whole time. It will be time for a sit-down, and your child may scream that he won't do it. You may ask if he's going to flush, since it's his job, and then face hysterical tears. First, don't panic and don't give up. Remember, your toddler is feeling the push-pull of wanting to be independent and wanting to be your baby, of wanting to please you and wanting to say no, of wanting to accomplish toilet training and feeling overwhelmed, all at the same time.

Try to figure out why the tantrum is coming now. Is she overtired or getting sick? Did a sibling just have a tantrum of his own, and now this one wants the attention? Understanding why the child is having this behavior will help you feel less angry in response. Then treat it as you would any other unwanted behavior. Tell your child that crying/screaming/kicking is not okay, that you know he is upset but will have to calm down. Then ignore the child until the tantrum resolves.

Your next action is vital. Try to give your child a choice, but not doing the job is not a choice offered. He can do the job now or in 5 minutes, or he can do it by himself or with your help. If you are using a reward system, tell your child that he will not earn his reward if he doesn't even try. Remember that you are teaching the child to cope with frustration and overcome challenges, not to give in when he feels overwhelmed.

There may be a time when nothing seems right. Your child may have become emotional and out of control about the hassle of learning to use the toilet. He may cry or throw a severe temper tantrum.

First, remember that it is okay, and that you can manage it. Temper tantrums are not novel. Most toddlers have three to five temper tantrums a day. Why would your child be any different? It goes with being a busy child.

When your child shifts into high gear with emotion, shift yourself into low gear. Don't desert your child by sending him to his room, and don't walk far away. But don't pay much attention to him, either. By being near him, help him by modeling calmness. The tantrum will pass.

It's important for you and your child to put your child's anger into understanding words. You can say something like, "I know doing your job of sitting on the toilet can be hard, but you can do it. When you're done being angry, then you'll need to sit on the toilet."

It's best for you to be prepared for temper tantrums. You don't want the temper tantrum to work for your child, getting him out of learning to use the toilet. Don't try to talk your child out of being angry. You'll only feed the anger that way.

Resist becoming angry yourself. If you let your emotions rise, the situation could turn ugly if you get angry, too. Just let your child's anger pass and then get back to the situation.

Keeping With It

Looking for small successes will help you and your child keep with the training. Celebrate each new skill, from the smallest step into the bathroom to the accidental poop into the toilet that surprised your child during a sit-down time. Make light of the momentary explosions, ongoing accidents, and occasional refusals. Make sure your child hears you tell your spouse or family about what jobs were done well, and don't mention the things that weren't done at all. Think back to where you started, and list all of the changes you and your child have made.

Reinforce the positive gains with statements like, "I'm proud of you for trying to poop on the toilet. I hope you're proud of yourself."

Deciding to Back Off

Parents sometimes wonder when to give in. If you're making small steps, just keep going. It may take longer than you expected, but we know what happened to the tortoise and the hare. On the other hand, if your child is getting nowhere at all, and there are only tantrums without new accomplishments, then deciding to back off may be reasonable. If an unexpected stress happens, such as the death of a loved one or a change in teachers, then don't expect your child to meet the challenge of toilet training at the same time. Tell the child that you know toilet training will happen, but let's think about it another time, since we are thinking about something else right now. Be sure to be clear the child isn't failing, but that we want to think about one thing at a time, and right now toilet training is not on top of the list.

If there's no stressor you can blame for interfering with the plan, then go back to Chapter 1 to figure out why the child is having so much trouble. If modifying your parenting, the child's diet, schedules, and clothing options are not helping enough, then skip to Chapter 9 for more ideas of what to do.

Think of it as giving your child the gift of time. Keep her in Pull-Ups full-time, and allow her mind, body, and emotions more time to mature. You can try again later, several weeks or a few months from now.

This is what Amy's mom did. She tried to potty train 2½-year-old Amy the first week in September, asking Amy to make her pee and poop on the toilet, but Amy wouldn't do it. Her mom made the same suggestions the first week in October.

The same thing happened again. Amy showed no interest, only to her mother's frustration. In November, there was another try, and still no progress. Then her mother tried something new. She put Amy in underwear for 2 hours each day again in December, but Amy would wet and then poop in her underwear.

Amy's mother changed her plan again the next month. Rather than aiming for dry and clean underwear or for all the poops and pees in the toilet, she offered Amy the choice of sitting on the closed toilet to practice making her poops, or trying the first wipe. Amy was much more successful with these new jobs, and was proud of her own accomplishments.

After several weeks and many jobs, Amy wanted to wear her princess panties when at home. Her mom would put Pull-Ups over her panties when they left the house, but she only did so for 2 weeks. After that, it was unnecessary, because Amy was fully trained.

The Least You Need to Know

- Build on the success of dry underwear.
- Slowly add small jobs that are part of the whole toilet training process.
- Small steps—from washing hands or flushing the toilet—can often be the first sense that the potty training will be successful.

- Recognize success, even if it's small.
- Sometimes during the potty training process, there are times when stress or other circumstances makes it necessary for the parents to back off.

Chapter 7

Making It Fun

In This Chapter

- Nagging, scolding, or punishing
- Using rewards and incentives
- Tapping into your child's imagination

A basic key for training the reluctant child is keeping it fun. That's easier said than done, especially when your child starts off with no interest in training or downright refuses to do it. Maybe you've even tried sticker charts in the past, only to find your child doesn't care one bit about earning a sticker.

How are a frustrated parent and reluctant child supposed to have fun toilet training? This chapter is full of ideas to keep your little one engaged and interested in potty training.

No Scolding, Reprimands, or Humiliation Allowed

When you're dealing with a reluctant child, it's important that you stay positive about potty training.

Some points for you to remember:

- Don't nag your child about toilet accidents in his or her underpants.

- Don't punish your child for accidents. Don't scold or yell about it, and don't take away favorite toys or play activities.

- Develop and maintain a "No Big Deal" attitude. When your reluctant one wets, just act as if it's no big deal. Clean up your child, and go on with the day.

- Always keep in mind that your child will outgrow this problem.

Your child needs your loving support to master this new potty skill, and when we learn any new task there always will be some setbacks. Encouragement is what the child needs. Keeping a positive attitude will go a long way.

Punishing your reluctant child for not using the potty correctly will add to the stress-load your child is carrying. This will be counterproductive, and won't help you or your child in the potty training process. Punishments make all of us recognize our errors and failures, and the goal in potty training is to highlight your child's successes.

Sometimes punishments around training are actually unfair. You really don't want to punish your child for doing something that isn't within his control. For example, if your child is afraid of using the bathroom, punishment for accidents is punishment for being scared. That's not fair: teaching the child to overcome the fear is a more helpful solution. You don't want to be a scary parent, and have your child living in constant fear of you.

Potty Do's

Reassurance and loving support always work best when training the reluctant child.

As you are working with your reluctant toddler, follow these guidelines:

- Watch your facial expressions. Your child is like a sponge, and is quick to absorb your negative looks and feelings.

- Be careful of your tone of voice. The least bit of difference from normal could be sending the wrong signal to your child.

- Check your body language, too. Crossed arms or a disgusted look could be telling your child of your dismay.

Reluctant children are often quite sensitive, and the slightest negative response can feel like a huge reprimand to them. Reprimanding your child, in any form, will simply not work.

Of all the things you could do wrong, humiliation is at the top of the list. It will not work, and will probably make things worse.

Have you ever been humiliated at work? Did it make you want to do a better job? Approach new challenges? Do extra work to please your boss? Probably not. You probably wanted to quit on the spot, or at least harbored resentment toward the guilty person forever. A humiliated child will feel much the same way. Your child might want to give up on potty training, too. Humiliation is the worst action, and something to avoid at all costs. If you realize after the fact that something you did or said embarrassed your child, apologize and reassure your child you won't do that again.

Potty Don'ts

Humiliation creates a whole new obstacle in itself for your child; she doesn't need any more stress than she already has.

You have to keep potty training fun. Before you try to add that fun element into your plan for a successfully trained, potty-using child, make sure you're not shooting yourself in the foot. Be positive and don't punish your child in any form—verbally, physically, or with body language.

When your child uses the potty to pee or poop, be enthusiastic about it. Pile on the praise. You want to keep a good thing going. Make sure your words and actions beam with pride as you talk about this accomplishment.

Using Enticements to Potty Train

On those frustrating days when nothing goes right with your potty training, you might be tempted to offer your little one $100 or the best gadget in the store. Anything she wants if she just uses the potty!

Save your money. Bribery isn't going to work, at least not on the grand scale. But there's good news. You can tantalize your toddler simply, inexpensively, and quickly. The result is often a potty trained child with less frustration.

Banners and Fireworks Displays Are Too Much!

There are some things you don't want to offer your child. They include the following:

- A trip to Disney
- A lot of money, such as $20
- Any toy she wants

Why not?

It's simple. You're placing too much pressure on your child. In your child's mind, the question is, "What could I do that's worth that amount?"

Imagine if the authors of this book were being paid 10 million dollars to pen these words (yes, we're worth it, as is the advice we offer!). But what would that have done to us as a writing team? It would have created tons of pressure! The question in our minds would be, "How can we make a toilet training book that good?"

Sooner or later, we would have developed a stifling case of self-doubt: besides solid advice, what do we have to offer worth that much?

Soon, we would have developed stress, anxiety, frustration, fighting, and a feeling of being overwhelmed. That's what a kid would feel like, too, if you try to bribe them with too large a prize for potty performance.

Using your imagination and a little creativity can have the effect you want, with far less expense and no stress on your child.

Start Sticker Charts

There are many advantages to using simple sticker charts. The benefits include the following:

- It's a small item.
- It's inexpensive.
- It's appropriate.
- It offers an immediate reward.
- Toddlers love them!

Give a sticker for each specific job. Sitting, wiping, flushing, and washing hands all deserve a sticker for each success. Praise the sticker chart and your little one's earned stickers! Small children love sticker charts. They love playing games, and enjoy winning. As they are successful, they get to place another sticker on their special chart.

Every few weeks, add new stickers. When there is a new job, add a new sticker. Keep changing them. Let your imagination go wild here.

Allow your child to choose from several stickers. This simple selection allows your child to have some control in the potty training process. Consider it a simple form of control.

Parents reading this section might have already tried stickers and be tempted to skip ahead. Wait! Sticker charts are different now from when you tried them in the past. Perhaps stickers were the prize for a job that was too hard, like making in the toilet. Now stickers are for a smaller, more manageable task. Last time, stickers may have been offered in the midst of tears, fighting, even punishments for accidents. Now that you've set the stage to only emphasize the positive, your child may be more open to this sticky incentive.

One of the questions you might have is where to hang this potty achievement chart. In the bathroom? On the fridge? The answer is simple: wherever you decide it is appropriate. Think about asking your child for some input. Respect your child's wishes as best you can.

Potty Do's

You can use your computer to make a special chart for your child. See Appendix B for a sample reward chart.

The allure of stickers eventually lessens for most kids. If that happens, you'll need to heighten the reward. You can try with new stickers, larger ones, or puffy, sparkly, touch-feely ones. At some point, stickers alone stop motivating lots of kids. At that point, you might change the deal, so that three stickers add up to earning a special treat.

Incentives

At some point and for some children, stickers will not do the trick. Rather than working for the accomplishment of an immediate sticker, some children do best with a different kind of incentive system.

Incentives are for slightly older children—4- to 5-year-olds who can start seeing more in the future.

Check Chart

For older kids, beyond stickers, you might try a similar chart but instead of placing stickers on it for doing the specified job, the child puts his own checkmark on the chart for each job done. Checks are a little more mature, for kids who think stickers are for babies, or for kids who lose interest in stickers. They get to mark their own checks off, and earn treats when enough checks end up on the chart. Start off with earning a treat for three checks, and then increase it to five. Here are some rewards that kids can earn for every batch of checks.

Lists of rewards for 3- to 4-year-olds and those 5 years and older:

- 3 to 4: M&Ms, a chocolate kiss, small cookie, grab-bag gift, extra story at bedtime, special time with parent
- 5 and older: same as above, extra TV or computer time, stay up 15 minutes later at night

Using Tokens for a Change

Quite similar to the check chart, this simple reward system allows your child to drop chips or tokens in a jar. You can use poker chips or any other small token (bingo markers, buttons, and so on). You just want to use something that makes a fun clank.

Use a clear bottle so your child can see it, and watch it fill with each addition. You want to use something that can safely be shaken so it makes noise. At first, just putting a chip in the jar may be reward enough for doing the job. Just like stickers, this becomes less motivating over time. When that happens, tokens should add up to a reward on the list. Older kids understand that tokens are like money; maybe three buttons lets your child buy a reward from the list you created together.

Creating Grab Bags

Every child loves the excitement of the unknown coupled with the surprise of a reward. Remember that it is not necessarily the item that is important, but the fun of the grab bag.

Wrap small dime-store items or place them in small brown paper bags. Place the items in a larger bag, basket, or box, and after a certain number of stars, stickers, checks, or tokens are earned, your child is allowed to pick something from the grab bag.

Pick items that are inexpensive and will be fun for your child. Some of the items you could place in the smaller bags are

- Gum
- Marbles
- Colored straws
- Small toys, such as a doll, action figure, or car
- New Lego piece
- Glittery crayon
- Photo of pet
- ChapStick
- Healthy snacks, such as a box of raisins

The idea here is to use whatever will make your little one smile and feel successful for using the potty properly. Younger kids who put things in their mouths should stay away from marbles, and won't be interested in ChapStick. ChapStick is a better choice for the older preschooler who wants to be like adults. Whether it be a small trinket or a wash-off tattoo, a grab-bag item serves as a reward. Reaching into a bowl or bag or basket to get the surprise will get your child excited about using the toilet. It may take several tries, but it will work.

Rewarding with Special Time

The most effective reward you can give your child is special, uninterrupted time. At first, it may seem like such a simple concept that it won't work. Nevertheless, parent time is the greatest reward of anything you can give to your child.

This special reward can be given for each check, token, sticker, or a group of three to five (you are in charge here, so you can set the rules). After earning whatever is required, the child is rewarded with special time with the parent.

You'll need to label the time together for your child. You probably spend a lot of time together already, so you want to distinguish this specific activity from the other times you're playing, chatting, and doing fun activities. Special time is an extra. It's a special reward that your child earned for doing the toileting job, so you have to make that clear. You could tell your child, "This extra

story/last game/_____ is because you did your
job of sitting/wiping/flushing/_____ so well
today. I am so proud of you."

Make a list of special time activities you can do
together. Some of the things might be

- An extra bedtime story
- A card game
- Bike ride at the park
- Playing a board game
- Walk after dinner
- A video together but alone from any other
  distractions

Use your imagination here to come up with what
those special times should be, and what your child
would like to earn as a reward.

Creating Your Child's Own Imaginative Story

Another way to make it fun: turn toileting or the
job of the week into part of a story that the child
makes up. This is an activity probably best for kids
over 4. Together you can make up a story and then
write a book based on the child's story. Guide your
child so there is a character doing a toileting job.

Next, read the book before it's time to do the job;
your child will "practice" it by reading it in the

story, and may feel more comfortable with the real-life challenge. Another option is to make up a story about something great that happened in the bathroom; for every sit-down time, think of a new thing that happened there. Maybe together you will think of a new place the poop or pee will go when it goes down the drain. You could also think of favorite characters that used this bathroom. Remember, the goal is to make it fun. Any laughing and smiles around the toileting topic will bring you closer to training your child.

Using Magical Thinking

Make-believe thinking is a new skill for kids at around 3 years of age. They start to make up explanations for things they can't see or don't understand. You might be seeing this in the form of elaborate pretend play, where your child uses dolls or action figures in activities with many steps. It may be based on real life, with figures eating dinner and going to sleep, but may include fantasy as well: dolls can fly, figurines can transform from one animal to another.

Try to use this new ability to help your child face toileting challenges. If she says it will hurt to poop when sitting down, suggest that wearing a dress and then lifting it up when she sits will make it easier to poop on the toilet. If he's afraid that he'll fall in, suggest that bringing a favorite toy or stuffed animal into the bathroom could help make sure he won't fall in.

Some kids insist that the poop won't come out. If you are sure the child isn't constipated, you need a way for the child to change this way of thinking. Arguing that the poop will come out probably won't be convincing, as you've likely figured out already. Suggest doing a special dance to make the poop come out more easily, and see if this helps your child change the "stuck" thinking.

You are already using magical thinking in the story you have written together. Chances are the story wasn't logical or real, but it was fun and reassuring. Your toddler or preschooler does not depend on rational and reality-based ideas—that's the fun of being a kid!

Harnessing the Power of Suggestion

In this book you're encouraged to follow the child's lead, but you may have to suggest where the magical thinking goes. Plant seeds in your child's fertile mind. Keep the stories upbeat with huge successes and happy endings. Have your child start with an idea, and then add to it in the direction you want it to go. Let's say you saw a turtle in a book. You might suggest your child make up a name for a new turtle, maybe "Turtle Tim." You could take the next step and say, "I bet Turtle Tim is a toilet flusher! Do you think he flushes fast or slowly?" If your child says, "Slowly!" you can take the next step, such as, "I think Turtle Tim flushes so slowly, he's the slowest flusher in the world! Isn't that funny?" Add other things Turtle Tim does slowly, and then act out his slow activities. Walk really slowly together, talk really slowly together, and flush the toilet really slowly. Before you know it, your child is accomplishing toileting tasks!

Bringing in Your Child's Alter Ego

Another way to incorporate magical thinking into toileting is by using an imaginary friend. Turtle Tim is like an imaginary friend, and lots of kids already have a pretend playmate. Have the "friend" do the job of the week first, to pave the way for your child. Together they can sing songs, read books, and sit on the toilet so that it's a little less overwhelming. The imaginary friend can do the job of the week (in your imaginations, of course) before your child does it himself. These invisible playmates can be reassuring and help children feel less alone.

The Least You Need to Know

- Scolding, humiliation, and punishment will not help train a reluctant potty user.
- Sticker charts serve as a great incentive for the child learning to use the potty.
- Create special rewards to entice your child to use the potty.
- Don't offer large rewards as incentives for training.
- Use your child's imagination to help with the potty training.

Chapter 8

Urine Trained, Not Bowel Trained

In This Chapter

- Why some kids pee but don't poop in the toilet
- When constipation plays a role
- How to treat constipation and when to get more help

At this point in your toileting plan, you might have made lots of progress. Stress around toilet training is hopefully down, or at least it's no longer obvious in front of your child. Small steps toward using the toilet might be evident—maybe there have been some successes, maybe your child is sitting, wiping, and washing completely independently. Many children may be using the toilet for urination pretty consistently; some may have been doing that for quite some time.

You're not alone if your toddler uses the potty to pee, but not for bowel movements. This is a very common problem, and there are solutions. Defecating *and* urinating in the potty is the goal. In fact, if all that's left is to help your little one actually get those poops in the toilet, most of the hard work is behind you.

Stool soiling isn't as scary as it first might seem. It doesn't mean there is something terribly wrong or unusual about your child. Don't despair, this chapter will help.

Avoiding Constipation

The most common reason children have trouble using the toilet for pooping is because they are constipated. Constipation doesn't mean that the child hardly ever makes a poop; it means that the poops often hurt or are hard to make. Kids can be constipated and make a poop daily, or kids can have comfortable, easily evacuated poops twice per week.

Constipation is common in children, and usually predates difficult toilet training. The typical scenario is that the child had at least one episode of constipation when it hurt to have a bowel movement. This can occur following an illness, when the child became constipated because of a medication, after a starchy meal, or during a vacation when regular schedules were disrupted.

After that painful poop, like anyone would, the child tries to avoid re-experiencing that pain, and holds in the poop rather than being eager to let it out. When their days are busy and full of activities, kids much prefer ignoring the need to poop, avoid having the pain of making, and keep on playing.

Constipation is problematic—a vicious cycle when you think about it. For your toddler, she tries to avoid the pain from passing a hard stool. And by waiting, poop backs up, gets bigger and harder, and then hurts even more when the bowel movement finally occurs. Every time kids have a painful poop, they try harder next time to hold it in, making it just more painful when it finally comes out.

If your child is able to control urine and use the potty to pee, but is having trouble with pooping, the first step is to determine whether making a bowel movement hurts your child; if it does, your child might strain, get red in the face, or even tell you it hurts. If that's the case, then reluctance to poop on the toilet is probably based on constipation.

Constipation can be particularly confusing if you see lots of poop in your child's Pull-Ups or underwear all the time. Sometimes what happens here is the child holds on to the stool, which builds up into a large ball or hard log (you may occasionally see these very, very, very large ones in the toilet!).

That hard, backed up, big poop stretches out the gut wall, and soft poop formed above it leaks around the constipated hard stuff. The leaky poop ends up as a mess in your child's underwear. It can be smears, hard balls, or even formed-looking stools. Stop and realize that your child has no control over this overflow poop. It's literally leaking out without warning, and your child can't control it while the constipated poop is still inside.

Potty Don'ts

Don't blame your child for poop accidents. Stool soiling is often from constipation, and that's fixable.

This might be the situation for a child who makes pees and some poops in the toilet but still has lots of poop accidents. In those cases, the children actually are toilet trained: they use the toilet whenever they can, it's just that a lot of the time they can't feel the leaky poop coming.

The underwear accidents have nothing to do with training or oppositional behavior, but have everything to do with constipation. Kids who wear underwear and are trained for urine but have poop accidents often hide soiled underpants under the bed or in a drawer. You'll figure this out pretty quickly.

Overflow accidents usually happen in older children, but the exact numbers of children who have the problem are not known: parents are reluctant to talk to anyone, even their child's pediatrician, about it. Many cases remain undocumented. The group of kids with overflow are really toilet trained and use the toilet for poop when they feel it coming and can hold it in, but when they have overflow accidents they soil their pants.

So, try to figure out which situation your child has. Is he refusing to toilet train because constipation makes it hurt? If that's the case, then you'll need to treat constipation as part of the toilet training plan. On the other hand, if your child can use the toilet sometimes, but at other times has leaky accidents, then you'll need a plan that treats constipation without working on the small steps of toilet training.

In all cases, constipation has to be treated if it's there.

You can't ignore the problem of poops that hurt, and you can't expect behavior changes alone to fix it. Kids can't necessarily just try harder to go. But this isn't the time to slack off on potty training, either! The constipation needs to be fixed either before you start working on toilet training steps or at the same time.

Remember, your child doesn't usually understand when or how poop accidents happened, and doesn't have the skills to make them stop with sheer effort alone. On top of that, he may be embarrassed and confused. Some kids get so used to the feeling and the smell that they really stop noticing it, which can be shocking and unbelievable to everybody else who is overwhelmed by the odor.

Training Trivia

Children who are difficult toilet trainers are more likely to be constipated than peers who train easily.

Bedwetting seems well covered in many parent magazines, but there is not much said about pooping in pants. You might have trouble finding advice about what to do from other sources.

Fortunately, constipation is usually not hard to solve.

Learning the Signs

You need to be on the lookout for constipation when your child is having trouble with bowel movements on the potty. Remember that your child is too young to understand what constipation is. It's up to you to detect the problem.

The first place to detect a constipation problem is to check the stools that are being made by your child. Your child's stools should not be any of the following:

- Less often than every three days
- Extremely large
- Small amounts of pellet-like stools
- Small bowel movements
- Very hard

Remember, constipation isn't about frequency, it's about how difficult it is for your child to empty the bowels.

Other signs of constipation include

- Distended or full-appearing belly
- Unwillingness to use the potty

- Abnormal loss of appetite
- Frequent complaint of bellyaches
- Hard straining while trying to make a bowel movement
- Bleeding from the rectum
- Unusual body language, such as clinging, hiding, or freezing

Potty Don'ts

Don't panic if you see blood. This is usually from a crack or tear of the skin near the anus (called a fissure). It's a simple and common condition that often accompanies constipation. If you see blood or a crack in the skin, see a doctor.

If your child is in daycare, there could be something about the environment that's part of the toileting reluctance. Is it easy for your child to get to the bathroom, or is it just easier to withhold pooping? It could be that your child just dislikes the whole idea of pooping at daycare.

From the strange bathroom to only being allowed to use the bathroom at specific times on a schedule, any number of factors at daycare could be interrupting the natural passing of the stool. Rather than going when the urge arises, the child may have to hold it in. In some kids this works just fine; others get backed up and constipated.

What You Can Do

Constipation problems are sometimes related to diet. Avoid foods that cause constipation, and increase foods that encourage bowel movements.

The simplest first step in solving constipation is to give your child more to drink. This will often soften the stools.

If the stools remain too firm, juice is one gentle option to soften them up. Apple juice twice a day is a good bet. If this doesn't work, try prune juice, which is even better. You can also add variety with peach or pear nectar juice drinks. Some of the products available contain sorbital, a natural laxative. Start with a cup or two a day. If you overdo it, you may have more poop come out at once than you hoped for! Your child might also get serious belly pain and gas.

Don't forget water. You can also give your child some milk, but don't overdo that, either. Some kids become constipated from too much milk.

A sure sign that you are giving your child enough fluids is the number of times per day your child pees. On average, a well-hydrated toddler should be peeing about every 3 hours throughout the day.

At the same time, readjust the balance of the foods in your child's diet to help. Foods that tend to cause constipation include:

- White bread
- Milk

- Pasta
- Cheese
- Bananas
- White rice

Cut back on those foods, and add foods to the diet that will help your child poop. Foods that tend to make bowel movements easier are:

- Fresh veggies (the more, the better!)
- Brown rice
- Fresh fruit (try to keep the skin on)
- Prune juice (this often helps the constipated child)
- Whole-grain, high-fiber cereals
- Whole-grain, high-fiber breads
- Fiber breakfast bars
- Popcorn

Keep in mind that your child needs fiber in his diet. Fiber is found in foods such as cereals, grains, fruits, and vegetables. If you have kept your child on baby food for too long, or feed your child a diet high in meat, fatty foods, or refined sugars found in candy and desserts, your child might not be getting enough fiber in his diet.

Raisins and dried prunes are another good snack to try. There is also fiber in peanut butter.

Potty Do's

Great snacks to give to your constipated toddler are fresh fruits, such as apples, grapes, apricots, plums, and berries.

Making these changes in your child's diet might be enough to stop the constipation problem. You will know that constipation is improved when stools are soft, formed logs that are easy for your child to make.

If your child remains anxious about pushing the poops out, since they have hurt so much in the past, then there are several other things you can try to make it easier to let them go. They include the following:

- **Give your child a warm bath.** Let her splash and play in the water with some toys. The warm water can stimulate the bowel and relax your child before making the poop.
- **Rub her belly.** The gentle massage could stimulate bowel movement and also reassure her that it won't be too hard.

After meals, it's time for your toddler to sit on the potty. Following eating and about 10 minutes of activity, get your child on the potty. Since typically a normal bowel movement occurs about 15 minutes after eating, this is a good time to catch the poop on the toilet.

Some reluctant children have been known to refuse to use the potty. Instead, they will go to the corner of a room, drop their pants, squat, and poop on the floor. Your first reaction, when you find it, is to go through the roof. There's a better course of action here.

When you make the discovery, lead your child to the spot, and ask for help in cleaning up the mess. Take the poop to the potty, and have your child watch what you do with it. Have your child flush the toilet. Then say, "there, the poop belongs in the potty." No yelling, no screaming. Remain calm. Hide your emotions. (We know, easier said than done.)

Continue your reinforcement of the expectation that your child will use the potty or toilet to make a bowel movement. It's not unusual for kids to insist on a diaper or Pull-Ups to make a poop. These kids are trained, just not for the toilet. Behave the same way you would if the poop were made on the floor: take the poop and the child, show the child that the poop must be flushed down the toilet, since that's where it belongs.

If your child asks for a diaper so she can soil in it, start by allowing it. However, her jobs are now geared to make steps from poop in the diaper to poop in the toilet. For instance, have her job be to make the poop in the diaper while standing in the bathroom. She then earns her sticker or treat for that.

A week or so later, have her make her poop while wearing the diaper but sitting on the toilet. With each job she does, she is closer to being toilet trained. Remember to give choices when you can: Which sticker to earn? Sit on potty or toilet? Diaper or Pull-Ups? She'll do a better job if she feels she has some control.

One other important point about constipation in your toddler: you cannot treat this as you would treat it yourself. Never give your toddler an enema, insert a suppository, or give a laxative without a doctor's advice or direction. As an adult, if you had the problem, you might take a laxative pill, and allow the problem to take care of itself. Treatment of young children with constipation is different from adults, so your doctor needs to be involved if you use anything more than diet as treatment.

When Bowel Retention Strikes

If you are not able to solve the constipation problem by yourself within 2 weeks, it's time to see the doctor. Of course, you might want to avoid all the suggestions presented here, and just go to the doctor. However, there are times when you need to take your child directly to the doctor:

- Your child is in extreme distress.
- There is a sign of blood in the stool.
- The stool has changed color and is now black.
- Constipation is recurring, and comes on quickly, despite a high-fiber diet.

If your child is constipated to the point that you take him to the doctor, it's not the time to panic. Constipation in children is common, and your health-care provider is probably very familiar with your concerns. If your child was potty trained and used the toilet to defecate, but now has stool accidents, it is probably because the bowel became impacted and there is now uncontrolled overflow. It happens. It will not be the first time the doctor has seen such a case.

When you meet with the doctor, this is not the time to be embarrassed or to hold back information. There are only a few things we don't talk about in our society, and pooping (and the lack thereof) is certainly on that list. That's why no one except the doctor has usually ever heard of the word *encopresis*.

Training Trivia

The medical term for stool soiling accidents is encopresis.

So it's time to dump on the doctor, so to speak. Be prepared to present all the facts. You and the doctor have the same goal: helping your child. Don't be surprised that even young children are often far from thrilled when having to tell the doctor about this.

Like you, your child realizes that poop accidents are embarrassing. Allow the child the chance to do any talking he wants, but offer to talk to the doctor for him, with him correcting you if you make any mistakes. After all, he may know more about his poops than you do.

Some of the things the doctor needs to know about your child's bowel movements are:

- Size
- Frequency
- Consistency

Not pleasant stuff to talk about, but necessary information for the doctor to evaluate. Write down as much as you can ahead of time—that record will help the doctor.

You also need to tell the doctor about the diet you have your child on, and the treatments you've tried. The doctor will need to know what medications your child has been taking, and whether they are related to constipation or are for other conditions. Don't forget any alternative vitamin or herbal treatments.

The doctor will use all the information you provide, as well as the physical examination, to determine how to solve the problem. One big factor for the doctor will be how old your child is and what you've done so far. The doctor will then decide on the proper way to proceed to solve the pooping problem.

Potty Do's

Be open with the doctor. Having a child who is constipated or having potty training problems doesn't make you a bad parent and doesn't make your child abnormal. The doctor is not there to be judgmental about your parenting skills. The fact that you're seeking professional help proves your concern for your child.

The doctor will also want to know your family history. Bedwetting runs in families, and if you are concerned about both stool and urine accidents, your doctor will want to know how your other children are doing. Some kids with constipation have bedwetting when the full bowel sits on the bladder during sleep and causes urine accidents, so to be thorough your doctor will want to know about urinary symptoms.

After compiling all the information, the physician may try a conservative approach to see if your child responds. The doctor might offer other suggestions and approaches to getting your tyke to use the potty.

For constipation, the doctor may start with diet suggestions, or she may suggest medication. There are lots of medications that come as liquids, syrups, tablets, and dissolving powders taken by mouth, sometimes mixed with food. This is usually done to get the little one to experience comfortable pooping so that he's less reluctant to make on the potty regularly.

The doctor might determine that your child has an impacted rectum. That sounds terrible, but it simply means your child's rectum is overloaded with poop. Not to worry—it sounds worse than it is to fix. Some providers recommend enemas for children who are very constipated or have an impacted rectum; this forces liquid into the colon to lubricate it and clean it out, and can quickly get rid of backed up stool. Sometimes a suppository is recommended; this is a small capsule (a pill) inserted in the rectum that helps the poop get squeezed out. These are fast fixes, but ones that the doctor should advise, and not the parent.

Any of these methods can clean out the impacted colon, and allow the stools to come out. If your child has been constipated for a long time, it may take more medication or a longer time to fully clean out the back-up.

If there is still no success, the doctor will start to look for more rare but still possible problems. These include such things as a urinary tract infection, neurological problems, or anatomical abnormalities. Such conditions are atypical, but are considered when straightforward treatment is unsuccessful.

Expect the doctor to ask questions about your child's behavior. Here again, honesty is the best response. If your little one is showing signs of disruptive behavior beyond just the toileting expectations, tell the doctor—don't cover it up. Toileting problems may be harder to treat in hyperactive, inattentive, and disruptive children. The doctor might try to solve the stooling problem while working on the larger behavioral issues.

Once your tot has an empty bowel, it's time to start the potty training again with all the energy you can muster. Get out those stickers. Get the doll. Get going!

Use the ideas already presented in this book. Watch the diet, and keep feeding your toddler the fruits, veggies, and drinks. Limit dairy products, and avoid too many potatoes. Be sure to do the sitting time on the potty after eating. Offer your encouragement, love, and lots of opportunities to have success in toileting tasks.

Even if there is no bowel movement, praise and reward your little one for sitting on the toilet and trying, or for doing whatever job was assigned.

It's Not What It Looks Like

Most children who have trouble with stooling on the toilet do not have an underlying emotional problem causing it. Studies tell us these kids don't have any more behavioral problems than any other children their age. In rare cases, however, there could be a psychological problem leading to your child's stool soiling. Some of the signs of this problem include:

- Soiling of pants every day despite treatment
- No medical or constipation problems
- Soiling of pants to draw parental attention
- Soiling of pants to control the situation, such as to avoid being with one particular person or in one particular situation

In those cases, bring your concerns to your medical provider immediately. A mental health professional might be needed to meet with you and your child to better understand what's going on. It could be a concerning emotional disorder, or it could be all about your child's temperament. For whatever reasons, your child is controlling the bowel movement and is telling you he wants or needs to maintain that control.

Temperamental issues are often tightly entwined with constipation. About 20 percent of the kids who refuse to use the toilet to stool have difficult temperamental traits. Know that you and your child are not alone with the problem.

When it's a temperamental problem, your patience is going to be tested daily. Try to remain patient, in control, and continue to approach the problem in a matter-of-fact way. It's often easier said than done. Remember, too, that humiliation is not going to work. For kids without a psychiatric or psychological problem but with truly difficult, stubborn, negative, oppositional tendencies, working with a mental health professional can still be helpful.

The plan should be to get your child's bowel movements back to normal, and to help him stop his poop withholding. The ultimate goal is to have him learn to control his bowels normally.

It's Not Your Child's Fault

Whether failure to train for poop in the potty is from constipation, overflow accidents, emotional or temperamental issues, none are your child's fault. The child can't just try harder to be good, since none of these are fully within his control. Remind yourself that the poop problem is neither your child's nor your own fault, but that you can work together to fix it.

The Least You Need to Know

- Constipation is a common problem for reluctant trainers.
- Constipation hurts, and your child might be holding in stools to avoid the pain.
- Constipation is sometimes cured with diet.
- Your child should be seen by a doctor if constipation persists.
- Stooling problems are never your child's fault, because the reasons for them are out of your child's control.

When Reluctance Leads to Resistance

In This Chapter

- Reducing stress on your child
- Seeking professional help
- Medical issues could be the problem
- Giving up control to others

Your toddler might be reluctant to potty train for any number of reasons. The reason for that reluctance could be the normal independence each toddler is developing, constipation that needs to be treated, or a power struggle between parent and child. Sometimes that reluctance develops into downright resistance—oppositional behavior that seems way out of proportion to what you expect from this child around toileting training. The degree of resistance may be directly linked to the underlying problem that is causing it.

Your child could be bedwetting, having daytime accidents, or unable to use the potty for bowel movements. Is it a case of stubbornness or defiance, or is there some other issue? Your challenge now is to figure out what is going on, and this chapter will help solve the mystery.

Let Go, Drop Back, Drop Out

There could be any number of reasons why your child is resisting using the potty with such vehemence. He needs to learn to dispose of his body waste properly, but for some reason, he just won't do it. Why he has dug his heels in and refuses to be potty trained is often perplexing.

To solve this problem, follow these steps:

1. Reread the first two chapters of this book.
2. Ask yourself: why is my child so reluctant?
3. Observe your child's behavior.

With this information, you can determine what to do. Maybe in your zeal to get started, you missed something in the first two chapters. Maybe it's as simple as changing the types of clothing your child is wearing, or switching to a potty rather than a toilet seat that attaches to the toilet.

Are you contributing to the stress with inadvertent pressure? Perhaps your approach is wrong. Stressing your child (or yourself) over your child's reluctance to use the potty is not going to help your reluctant child. If you sense stress, it's time to make changes to your approach.

Potty Do's _____

Be on the lookout for pain. Keep a watchful eye on your child while she tries to urinate or make a bowel movement. If there are signs of pain, make a doctor's appointment.

Just about all young children have temper tantrums. Beyond the occasional meltdown, watch for signs that his is a bigger or more concerning problem. Here are some hints that your child's tantrums are more than part of a typical developmental stage:

- They frequently occur several times daily.
- They are dangerous to the child: he becomes bruised, bleeds, puts himself in harm's way (takes risks in traffic, falls down stairs).
- They are dangerous to others: you or siblings are bruised, bleeding, or have broken bones.
- He is hysterical, does not calm within a few minutes, or seems out of control and wild.
- He is aggressive, purposely hurtful to others and wanting to cause harm, beyond the harm caused by thrashing and needing to be contained.

Some children who are having trouble training have Attention Deficit Hyperactivity Disorder (ADHD). It's a condition that becomes apparent in some children in the preschool and early school years. It's hard for these children to control their behavior and pay attention. Kids with ADHD may be harder to potty train, since they often have trouble sitting still and finishing tasks they start. Approximately 7.5 percent of children have ADHD, or about 2 million children in the United States. This means that in a typical classroom of 25 to 30 children, it's probable that at least one child will have ADHD.

If there is a history consisting of trauma or abuse, your child may also be difficult to potty train. Chronic family stress may significantly curtail the training.

Make an Appointment with the Doctor

If any of those situations might be true for your child (tantrums beyond expectations, ADHD, trauma, significant family stress), you will need your doctor's involvement. These additional concerns will have to be addressed for your child to succeed in training.

Another sign that it's time to make a doctor's appointment is if progress has been poor. Have there been any signs of progress? After 6 to 8 weeks, there should be some signs that your child is learning to use the potty. There should be some interest in using the potty. There should have been some successes, if not in using the toilet then at least in accomplishing some of the toileting jobs. But what if there are no signs of progress: not even occasionally doing the job, no change in attitude, nothing?

It's time to see the doctor. Start with the pediatrician.

After setting the appointment, get yourself and your child prepared. You need to be able to describe your child's bowel patterns, urination patterns, and any urinary or constipation symptoms. Make notes so you can tell the doctor what is going on. The more information, the better and easier it will be for the pediatrician to focus on the problem.

You should prepare your child for the visit, too. Tell your child that you're both going to the doctor for help, and that your child is not in trouble. Be sure to give your child lots of hugs, smiles, and kisses.

 Potty Do's

Be sure to keep a watchful eye on your child. Look for abnormal signs, such as cloudy urine, blood when wiping, or pain with urination or defecation. Report any such observations to the doctor.

Be positive with your child as you discuss the pending doctor visit. Say something like, "Let's go see Dr. Jones. She sees lots of kids. I bet she can give us some ideas to help you learn to pee in the potty."

Your child might be thinking he did something bad, and that's why he is going to the doctor. Children often ask if they will need a shot. Tell the truth. "You're not in trouble. It's just that we haven't figured out how to use the toilet yet. The doctor probably knows some way to help. We just want some new ideas." If your child asks about shots or needles, say that you don't know for sure but think there probably won't be any.

Another bit of information that will help the doctor is for you to provide your child's schedule. This should include your child's fluid intake, urination frequency, bowel movements, and sleep patterns. The doctor will also need to know about your child's food consumption.

Expect the doctor to ask probing questions like …

- Are there stressors at home?
- What does the urine looks like, what's the frequency, and when does it usually occur?
- Is there any family history of bedwetting?
- Do accidents happen when your child is too busy playing?
- During tantrums, does your child have accidents?

Based on the information you provide, along with an examination, the doctor will determine what the next step is. Usually children require only an extensive history and physical exam. However, the doctor will want to take a good look at the vagina or penis, and anal region. All children with daytime urine accidents and bedwetting will probably need to give a urine sample so the doctor can look for a urinary tract infection.

Seeking Professional Help

Usually, the problem of reluctance to use the potty is not a psychological, medical, or anatomical abnormality. However, rarely there are concerns to be investigated. For example, a child with an ectopic ureter (the tube that's supposed to go from the kidney into the bladder ends outside the bladder instead) leaks pee all the time.

Some children have blockages interfering with urine as it is passed out of the body: children with this problem have urinary incontinence but also may have to push hard to get urine out and have an abnormal urine stream. Another rare situation is the child with a problem of the spinal cord. Those children stretch their spinal nerves as they grow, and then have abnormal neurological function as they get taller, such as trouble with continence, motor coordination, and pain. All of these may sound terrible, but until you find out what's wrong, your child won't get the treatment available.

Daytime accidents may call for the doctor to make a diagnosis of an unstable bladder. The treatment may be relatively easy. Medication that relaxes the bladder may be prescribed. Some doctors may decline any long-term drug use for the daytime urination, preferring instead for the child to out-grow the problem.

Training Trivia

The commonly used medication for nighttime bedwetting is desmopressin or DDAVP. It is available in both tablets and nasal spray. It works well with children who seem to be producing too much urine that overflows from the bladder. The drug reduces the amount of urine produced during the night.

If the doctor suspects a urinary tract infection, a urine sample is needed. The treatment is anti-biotics.

Recurring constipation could also be the problem. See Chapter 8 for more information.

The doctor may order more specialized studies to look for anatomical or neurological problems. If one of these conditions is diagnosed, treatment options include medication and surgery.

Another possibility is the presence of a disease such as diabetes or epilepsy. If a diagnosis is made, treatment of the disease can often resolve the potty training issue.

Potty Don'ts

Don't demand a medication to fix your child's problem. While it might seem like the fastest and easiest solution, stop and listen to what the pediatrician is telling you. There may be other, better treatments than medication.

The pediatrician may also refer your child to another medical specialist if constipation can't be treated, if there is no development of the sensation of the "need to go," or if there is constant wetness.

Your child may need to see a mental health specialist if there is a lack of progress from a psychiatric disorder (such as anxiety) or trauma. Your child might have a case of persistent defiance of sufficient degree to be diagnosed as Oppositional Defiant Disorder (ODD). Children with ODD have a pattern of extremely hostile and noncompliant behavior characterized by anger, frequent arguing, spitefulness, and irritability. All children can have some of these traits some of the time, but children with ODD have such disturbances in behavior that learning and friendships are impaired.

Help your child overcome the obstacles. If you think your child might have ODD, in addition to seeking professional help, try these approaches:

- Minimize the number of orders you issue.
- Discourage whining or yelling. Model more appropriate ways to communicate frustration and anger.
- Make sure your child knows your expectations.
- Give your child hugs and kisses.

Relinquish Your Control

If your reluctant child is merely defiant without any more concerning medical, anatomical, or psychiatric issues, then the only way for you to remain in control may be to relinquish your control. If you are in the potty training struggle, you're not going to win. You may need to just let go. Encourage your child to be in control of the potty use, while you simply remain supportive and cheerful.

Generally speaking, most kids have bladder control by the time they are 2½ years (30 months) old. If your child is older, defiant, has no medical issues, and is still resisting, it's time to change tactics.

Switching Parent Jobs

Another option when nothing is working is to try switching jobs as parents. For whatever reason, this

might be the solution. It may eliminate an un-
healthy dynamic. Have the other parent do the
training while you step out. This could break the
current unsuccessful cycle.

You could be making your child feel stress, even
unintentionally. The other parent could provide
the fresh start your child needs.

The other parent might be a touch more lenient,
a tad more willing to allow the child to make decisions, or be better able to hide frustration or stress.
"Do you want to wear your red or blue shorts
today?" might be the style of the other parent,
while the first picks the shorts, or asks the same
question but indicates a preference without trying.
Little things can send big messages to your toddler.
Your child's life might be regimented for her.
Relax, and consider turning the reins over to the
other parent.

Potty Don'ts

It won't be easy to let go and give your
child's training to the other parent. Step-
ping back when your child is having a
tough time is difficult. Don't feel guilty or
ashamed. It might be what's best for your
child.

Engaging Teachers and Grandparents

Consider seeking help from your child's daycare teachers and grandparents during this difficult period. Just as you are having the other parent take over the potty training responsibility, engage the other adults providing care to do the same thing. By giving the job to the teacher, grandparents, or caregivers, it might be just enough to do the trick.

Offer Control in Other Areas

The more your child feels he's in control of the potty learning process, the faster he will decide to try to use it. Help your child build confidence by giving him control in other areas of his life. Allow him to choose his clothing, his breakfast food, or what toy to play with.

"Do you want to eat a banana or grapes for your snack?" does more than resolve the snack issue. It proves that you trust your little one enough to make decisions.

The Least You Need to Know

- Backing off and reducing stress may make the difference.
- Professional help may be needed to help your child train.
- Don't ruin your relationship with your child over potty training, but instead allow the other parent to handle the potty training.

The Bottom Line

In This Chapter

- Developing a potty training plan
- Potty training infants
- Having fun during potty training

By now, you are probably a potty guru. You're only on this page in the book—the first one of the last chapter—because you're either bored, or at your wit's end. Maybe you're looking for the last bits of potty wisdom. If you're here because you're desperate, reread the book slowly, talk to your child's doctor, or just put it away for a month or two.

As your own potty expert, you know what it takes to get your tyke to tinkle in the potty. You know that your child has the skills to make poops in the toilet, rather than in a diaper.

There's something mildly amusing about all of this, you know. Soon this book will be placed on the shelf, your little one potty trained and going on to other exciting things in life, like learning to read, having a best friend, rollerblading, and playing soccer.

But if you're reading this chapter because you want every bit of knowledge you can squeeze out of this book, please read on.

Having a Plan

Potty training the reluctant child is really a 4- to 6-month plan. Much like General Patton studied maps before moving his columns of tanks, men, and supplies, you must plan your moves. An easier child may be trained in a day, but let's face it, that's just not happening for you. From acquiring Pull-Ups®, the right potty chair, and implementing a plan of action, you are your own general in the field of potty training. You know your little soldier can do it, but needs your leadership, support, and strategy.

There are good and bad days, as well as good and bad weeks. There are successes, and there are those times when you wonder if your little one will be trained before he's a freshman in high school.

Getting yourself ready for potty training is probably as important as getting your child ready. From reading this book, you know that a lot of potty training is about behavior modification: not only your child's behavior, but also yours. You know that to train this particular kid, you have to change your approach, going more slowly than you ever imagined, and being unbelievably careful to be nothing other than loving and supportive of your little potty learner.

Your plan has to include ...

- **Setting up the training area.** The bathroom has to be child-friendly. It has to feel safe, secure, and be a place where your toddler can feel comfy. It needs a potty your child likes and can use easily, and a special place for your child's progress chart. A place for a basket of books or toys is also needed. The bathroom has to become one of the best places in the house.

- **Maintaining a "can do" attitude.** Your expectation is to meet very small new tasks, one at a time, rather than your previous hope for a poop in the potty right off the bat. You do this with your positive attitude and constant reinforcement of one little success after another.

- **Allowing your child to set the pace.** Your child will set the speed of the potty training, not you. Some children move more slowly than others. That's life. You have to go with the flow, so to speak. It's probably not your pace, but then again, it's not your poop.

- **Holding your tongue.** You need to keep your frustrations to yourself, and never show anger or disappointment. That's easier said than done, but it's what your child needs. And you will also never compare your child to another. Oh, it's okay to be tempted to do so, and you can think it, but you will never say it aloud to your child.

● **Going with your instincts.** A lot of potty training is just you going with your common sense. If your child is having a bad day, back off on the training. If your child is almost there, you keep going. When things aren't right, you consult your child's doctor. If poops aren't regular, you change the diet. Trust your instincts.

Potty Training Infants

There's a lot of talk about potty training infants. Some parents work on training even more slowly than we are recommending, and for all children. Recent media reports say that some parents are now toilet training from birth.

"The first day she peed on the potty she was 4 days old," one proud mother boasted on national television. Called "elimination communication," parents read their babies' signals and put them over the toilet when the poop or pee is coming. This form of early toilet training is practiced in scores of countries around the world.

Spurred on by contacts created via the Internet, several thousand people across the country have joined chat groups and e-mail lists to learn more about the techniques of encouraging a baby that's too young to walk or talk to go in a toilet. A nonprofit organization, Diaper Free Baby, has established over 75 local groups in 35 states to support parents in the practice. This new trend of infant potty training does not come without controversy.

Children have no control over their bladder or bowel movements for their first year, and only a little more control for the next six months. Everyone agrees it is not the child demonstrating control over the toileting. For some kids, however, it may help them slowly develop more awareness of their body signals from a younger age. It may prevent them from developing toilet refusal, if they have become used to being in the bathroom. But for some kids, it may be a stressful experience, being expected to evacuate on the toilet when they really don't have the skills. Pediatricians generally advise looking for signs of child readiness before beginning the training process. This includes 3-hour periods of dryness, identifying the urge to go, and having the language skills to communicate.

While communication between parents and the child should always be encouraged, there are lots of ways to bond. For most other areas of development, early encouragement is about learning less-complex skills before moving on to the bigger ones. In other words, we start by encouraging the child to roll, then sit, then crawl, then stand, then take steps, and then walk. We don't typically begin by walking the child ourselves, getting him familiar with it for when he can walk independently.

Early toileting skills to be encouraged could include promoting positive associations around pooping, celebrating the feeling of a clean diaper, teaching flushing and hand washing to 1- to 2-year-olds, and more generally focusing on confidence. All of these will support success when toilet training begins.

For more information about elimination communication, visit www.diaperfreebaby.org.

Making Potty Training Fun

Potty training should be fun and exciting, for you and your little learner. It's a big step in your little one's life. Sure, your child needs your help, but it is something that should be filled with excitement, some joy, and fun.

It's a time for you to communicate with and enjoy your child. Talking about pees and poops may not be the most pleasant topic in the world to you, but it's an important one, and it's generally a funny one for kids. Your child is going to use the toileting skills throughout life, and your goal is to make them routine and achievable.

Make the experience as much fun as you can. Focus on the successes, and look at the messes as just a routine chore. Have fun enjoying your toddler's enthusiasm and excitement over adding stickers to the progress chart. Laugh at the idea of those pees with the toddler. This should be a fun time in your life as a proud parent of that growing child of yours.

Laugh a lot, on the pot.

Don't frown, it's only brown.

Hang in there, it will get done.

It only helps if you make it fun.

And remember, it's only potty training.

The Least You Need to Know

- Develop your own plan for potty training.
- Trust your instincts and use common sense when developing your potty training plan.
- Training your infant to potty train is not really possible.
- Keep your sense of humor about potty training.

Resources

Websites

www.healthsystem.virginia.edu/internet/
pediatrics/patients/Tutorials/Constipation/
home.cfm
University of Virginia's website about encopresis
(stool accidents in children). Contains graphics
and explanations about stooling problems that are
useful for parents and children.

www.nationalparentingcenter.com
The National Parenting Center site offers a
newsletter and online chat rooms where you can
speak with other parents about potty training
issues.

www.babiesonline.com
Offers baby information, coupons, and freebies.

www.parenting.com
Site has lots of resources for parents.

www.parentsplace.com
Part of iVillage, offers information about babies.

Books

Bennett, Howard J., M.D. *Waking Up Dry: A Guide to Help Children Overcome Bedwetting.* Can be purchased through the American Academy of Pediatrics. (www.aap.org)

Brazelton, T. Berry, M.D., and Joshua D. Sparrow, M.D. 2004. *Toilet Training: The Brazelton Way.* Cambridge, MA: Da Capo Press.

D'Ippolito, Elaine. 2002. *Dry All Day Potty Training Skills Workbook.* Silver Spring, MD: 3D Publishing.

Frankel, Alona. 1999. *Once Upon a Potty—Boy.* New York: HarperFestival.

———. 1999. *Once Upon a Potty—Girl.* New York: HarperFestival.

Gomi, Taro, and Amanda Mayer Stinchecum (Translator). 1993. *Everyone Poops (My Body Science).* LaJolla, CA: Kane/Miller Book Publishers.

Goodman, Susan E., and Elwood Smith (Illustrator). 2004. *The Truth about Poop.* New York: Viking Juvenile.

Wolraich, Mark L., M.D., Editor-in-Chief, with Sherill Tippins. *Guide to Toilet Training.* Can be purchased through the American Academy of Pediatrics. (www.aap.org)

Zweiback, Meg. 1998. *Keys to Toilet Training (Barron's Parenting Keys).* Hauppauge, NY: Barron's Educational Series.

Sample Reward Chart

Little rewards can make a big difference to your child. They can help provide the incentive your child needs to learn the important steps in potty training. Use stickers to enhance the excitement of your child's progress.

Potty Chart

Monday					

Tuesday					

Wednesday					

Thursday					

Friday					

Saturday					

Sunday					

Fill in the box with sticker or a happy face every time
your little one does a Poo-Poo or a Pee-Pee successfully!!!!!!

The Trained Child: Nighttime Bedwetting and Daytime Accidents

Nighttime Bedwetting

Once children are toilet trained by day, parents often expect them to be dry at night as well. Not always. Kids can take months to years between being trained by day and having all dry nights. By five years of age, 85 percent of children are dry at night. After that, 15 percent of kids naturally will outgrow bedwetting every year. Doctors don't know exactly why some children take longer to wake up dry. Sometimes children make more urine during the night than their bladders can hold; many bedwetters are hard to arouse from sleep, either by a noise or a full bladder. When they don't wake, they wet accidentally.

Most kids are surprised to learn that bedwetting runs in families. In fact, half of kids with bedwetting have another member of the immediate family with a history of wetting, and almost three quarters have someone in the extended family with that history. After feeling embarrassed about the wet bed, finding out about relatives with the same problem can make a child feel much better.

If your child has never been dry at night, there may not be much you can do before age seven. It's important to review your concerns with your child's doctor, especially if your child also has daytime symptoms (frequent need to urinate, urine accidents, pain with urination). In many cases, a urine sample will be requested to be sure there is no urine infection. Constipation can make it hard to stay dry at night, so that will have to be considered as well. A bowel full of stool takes up too much room for the bladder to fill, so urine can't be contained during the night until the bowel is cleaned out.

After the doctor's visit, you may start planning for some behavioral interventions that will help your child stay dry. These will only be effective if your child is motivated to stop wetting. Limit fluids after dinner to minimize the amount of urine in the body. Be sure your child tries to urinate before bed. Some parents partially awaken a child to use the toilet before the parent goes to bed, between 10 and 12 at night.

A motivated child may be encouraged by small rewards in the morning for a dry bed, such as stickers or small treats. Once a child is seven or so, helping the child feel more control over the body and more awareness of its signals might help. Before bedtime, reading books, telling stories, and drawing pictures that focus on staying dry can help the child contain the bladder when sleeping.

If simple interventions don't work, your doctor may suggest a toilet training alarm. This gadget buzzes or sounds when your child's underwear are wet, and then your child will have to try to empty the rest of the urine into the toilet, change underwear, and replace the alarm. When used nightly with behavioral supports, bedwetting alarms can eliminate bedwetting for 80 percent of children. However, they do take a lot of time and energy on your part and on the part of your child.

For children who are really distressed about bedwetting but don't respond to any of the aforementioned interventions, your doctor may prescribe medication. DDAVP or desmopressin is a commonly used medication that decreases the volume of urine produced in the night. It works about 60 percent of the time, and once you stop the medication, the urine accidents will come back. If your child takes DDAVP, don't allow more than one cup of fluids after bed, as there is a risk of electrolyte abnormalities developing and causing seizures. There are other medication options, but they are more controversial or have greater risk potential.

Daytime Accidents

Some children are toilet trained while still having daytime urine accidents. When they feel the urine coming and can hold it in until they get to the bathroom, they do so. However, in between voids on the toilet they have drips, leaks, or full-blown urine accidents they can't control. For these children, reluctance is not the problem. If they could pee into the toilet, they would.

In this scenario, start by talking to your pediatrician. Again, a urine sample may be checked, along with a thorough physical examination. Constipation will be considered, since a full bowel can irritate the nearby bladder so it empties suddenly. Constipation treatment will fix that situation. Your doctor will refer your child to a specialist if there are concerns for anatomical, neurological, or medical problems causing the daytime urine accidents.

Bladder strengthening exercises may be prescribed, meaning your child will stop and start the urine flow when in the bathroom. Many children will need a schedule for urination, going to the bathroom every two hours or so to empty the bladder before the accident happens. Occasionally, medication can relax the bladder wall to treat daytime accidents. In some cases, your child will only need time to outgrow this problem.

The Top 16 Questions About Potty Training

Question 1

My son was fascinated with his potty when we first got it, but now he won't go near it. He screams and yells if I ask him to just sit on it. Now what should I do?

First, take a toileting break. After things calm down, give him a choice of sitting with the toilet seat down or with his pants on. Give him a small treat for doing this job.

Question 2

Should we be concerned with our daughter's potty mouth? Now she is saying things like, "I can pee-pee with my wee-wee on you" or "You're a big stinky poop."

Don't be concerned, but try to modify her language by modeling more appropriate talk. She is being a normal toddler, testing limits to see what she can get away with. Be clear that certain comments are unacceptable, and give her another phrase to express her feelings.

Question 3

My child wets the bed at night or has a bowel movement. Should I be concerned?

Children who have stool accidents are often constipated. This can cause bedwetting, too. Speak to your child's doctor about this. There may be some simple solutions.

Question 4

My son was excited about wearing big kid underpants, but now he wants his diapers on. What should I do?

Work on a different job in toilet training. For example, allow him to practice flushing the toilet and washing his hands. Let him experience some successes to build up confidence.

Question 5

How much bribery or rewards are too much?

Daily jobs are worth stickers or small items. A week's worth of jobs is worth a small toy or video rental. Incentives should always be specific and limited, not "any toy you want."

Question 6

Should I buy my son a urinal, in addition to the potty chair?

No. Most homes have toilets only, and boys can learn just fine to urinate into a toilet standing up.

Question 7

What is your recommendation about taking a child into a public rest room? How old should my son be before I allow him to go in the bathroom by himself?

This very much depends on where you live and where the public place is located. Children under 8 should always be accompanied. If you are in any doubt, accompany your child.

Question 8

My son seems ready to be potty trained. All the signs of readiness are there. How long should it take?

Easy kids can train in a day, reluctant kids can take several months.

Question 9

My daughter tries to use the potty. Then she gives up, pulls up her Pull-Ups, and within a few minutes, she is wet. What should I do?

Work on a goal other than "using the potty" so she develops some confidence. For example, have her sit on the potty in her Pull-Ups to urinate, to get her one step closer to being trained. If this persists despite motivation on her part, talk to your doctor.

Question 10

My child is a messy wiper. What can I do to improve the wiping skill?

Use flushable disposable wipes. They are better cleaners. Some kids with weaker fine motor coordination might take a longer time to become adept at wiping.

Question 11

My child seems to sit on the potty for a long time, before finally going. Dilly-dallying might be the right words to describe this. What should I do?

Nothing. As long as he is using the toilet, celebrate. Adults often linger on the toilet as well. If that's the way he likes to go, or if he needs that time to relax, let him. You may need to modify the schedule around that (wake up earlier, eat breakfast later).

Question 12

My child was almost potty trained, but now wets herself almost daily. Why is she doing this?

Talk to your doctor. This could be signs of a urinary tract infection or constipation. Also, think about other stresses in her life. Children often regress when they are upset or overwhelmed about something.

Question 13

My husband pees with the toilet seat up. Should I teach our son to train that way?

The toilet seat can either be up or down when a boy first trains. Starting with it down can remove the steps of raising it and lowering it when a child starts pottying, but it also increases the area where the child aims. If you aren't sure which choice to make, ask your son what he prefers.

Question 14

Is it okay for my older child to teach my younger child how to potty train?

Yes, as long as it's okay with each child. Older kids often enjoy being the teacher, and younger ones often love mimicking the older one. On the other hand, your leader shouldn't feel responsible for the little one's developmental progress, and the youngster shouldn't have to answer to the big kids.

Question 15

We told my child that peeing in the yard is an acceptable option if it's hard to "hold it in," and then we saw a stool on the grass. What should we do?

Don't worry. Urination and defecation have slightly different social meaning to adults, differences that children may not appreciate. Just clarify that making pees outside is fine but poops are different, and belong in the Pull-Ups, potty, or toilet.

Question 16

My child will not sit on anyone else's toilet, and I can't realistically bring our potty or seat everywhere we go. Any other ideas?

A relatively new product is called a potty hammock. It slides over the toilet seat and tightens, preventing direct contact with the toilet and giving more support by narrowing the hole. Look for it at http://mypottyhammock.com.

Index

K-L-M

N-O

P-Q

U–V

underwear
 changing from dia-
  pers, 77-78
 shopping for with
  child, 39-40
 starting two hours per
  day, 82-85
unsolicited advice, 64-67
urinary tract infections
 (UTIs), 14

videos, parent training,
 19-21

W–X–Y–Z

wardrobe
 changing from diapers
  to pants, 75-76
  cotton training
   pants, 77
  example, 79-80
  Pull-Ups, 76-77
  underwear, 77-78
 eliminating difficult
  clothing, 74-75
websites, Diaper Free
 Baby, 158